Past Masters
General Editor Keith Thomas

The Buddha

Michael Carrithers is Lecturer in Anthropology at the University of Durham and author of *The Forest Monks of Sri Lanka* (also published by OUP).

Past Masters

Forthcoming

Michael Carrithers

The Buddha

Oxford   New York

OXFORD UNIVERSITY PRESS

Oxford University Press, Walton Street, Oxford OX2 6DP

Oxford New York Toronto
Delhi Bombay Calcutta Madras Karachi
Kuala Lumpur Singapore Hong Kong Tokyo
Nairobi Dar es Salaam Cape Town
Melbourne Auckland Madrid

and associated companies in
Berlin Ibadan

Oxford is a trade mark of Oxford University Press

First published 1983 as an Oxford University Press paperback
and simultaneously in a hardback edition

British Library Cataloguing in Publication Data

Data available

Library of Congress Cataloging in Publication Data
Carrithers, Michael.
The Buddha.
(Past masters)
Bibliography: p.
Includes index.
1. Gautama Buddha—Biography. 2. Buddhists—India—
Biography. I. Title. II. Series.
BQ822.C37 1983 294.3'6 83-8004
ISBN 0-19-287589-2 (pbk.)

9 10

Printed in Great Britain by
Biddles Ltd
Guildford and King's Lynn

To Elizabeth

Preface

Until the present century the Buddha was probably the most influential thinker in human history. His teaching prospered throughout the subcontinent of India for more than 1500 years, and in that time it changed and diversified at least as much as Christianity did in its first 1500 years in Europe. By the thirteenth century AD, when the power of Buddhism was broken in its original home, it had long since spread to Tibet, Central Asia, China, Korea, Japan and Sri Lanka, and it was making its way into South-East Asia. Buddhism's history in those countries was as complicated as it had already been in India.

I have not attempted to explain such a vast matter in this short book. I have only recounted the life of the Buddha and described the genesis and significance of his teaching. I have tried, however, to phrase this account so the reader will be able to see why Buddhism moved so easily across continents and survived so well through the centuries.

Contents

Note on quotations

Abbreviations
References to works in the Buddhist canon are to the Pali Text
Society editions of the Theravāda canon. The letter refers to
the appropriate *nikāya* (collection), the first number to the
volume within the *nikāya*, and the second number to the page
in the volume. Thus a reference to the *Majjhima Nikāya*,
second volume, page 91 would be written M II 91. Where I
have referred to a whole discourse I have given the number of
the discourse, e.g. M I no. 15. The following abbreviations are
used:

D   *Dīgha Nikāya*
M   *Majjhima Nikāya*
A   *Anguttara Nikāya*
S   *Saṃyutta Nikāya*

Other references are to the *Udāna* (U) and the
Paramatthajotikā (P), also in Pali Text Society editions;
and to the *Bṛhadāraṇyaka Upaniṣad* (B) and the
Chāndogya Upaniṣad (C), which are cited giving book,
chapter and section number so that any edition may be
consulted.

Translations and Terms
The translations are almost entirely my own. Anyone who
wishes to trace citations to their context will find that the Pali
Text Society's English translations are keyed so that one may
light more or less on the appropriate passage, though one's aim
is better if one can consult the Pali. A little experimentation
will be necessary.

The technical terms are in Pali, except where I have noted that they are in Sanskrit.

Pronunciation

To avoid really embarrassing mistakes in Pali pronunciation it need only be borne in mind that *c* is equivalent to English *ch*, so *cetanā* is pronounced very roughly chay-tuh-naa; and that *h* after a consonant means only an extra breathiness in pronunciation, as in the English pi*th*ead or dog*h*ouse. Those wishing to pronounce *Buddha* correctly will need to know that the doubled *d* is pronounced as such, rather as doubled consonants are pronounced in Italian. Thus it is roughly Bud-dhuh, *not* Booduh.

The special symbols that appear above or below certain letters in Pali and Sanskrit words transliterated in the text affect the pronunciation of those letters *roughly* as indicated in the following table of equivalence:

ā	*ah*
ś	half-way between *s* and *sh*
ñ	*ny* as in ca*ny*on
ṭ ḷ ṇ	instead of the tongue touching the back of the teeth, as in English, it is taken further back towards the roof of the mouth
ṣ	*sh*
ṃ	*ng*

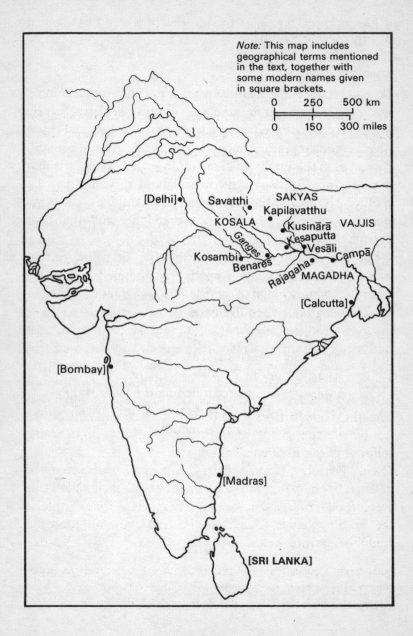

Note: This map includes geographical terms mentioned in the text, together with some modern names given in square brackets.

0   250   500 km

0   150   300 miles

[Delhi]•   Savatthi•   SAKYAS
               Kapilavatthu•
KOSALA   •Kusinārā   VAJJIS
          Ganges   Kesaputta
                          •Vesāli
Kosambi•   •Benares•   Campā•
          Rajagaha•   MAGADHA

[Calcutta]•

[Bombay]•

[Madras]•

[SRI LANKA]

1 Introduction

Among the ruins of Anuradhapura, the ancient capital of Sri Lanka, there rests alone on a pedestal above the grass a seated image of the Buddha in stone, slightly larger than life. The statue is conventional, probably more than a thousand years old, of a type found throughout Buddhist Asia. The legs are folded in meditation, the hands laid one upon the other in the lap. Buddhists hold that it was in this posture, seated beneath a tree more than 2500 years ago, that the Buddha was awakened, attaining decisive knowledge of the human condition and the unshakeable certainty that he was released from its suffering.

In its excellence, however, the Anuradhapura image is far from conventional. The back and head are disciplined and upright; but the arms are relaxed and the face reposes in tranquillity. The figure seems intelligent and serene, wed perfectly to the unmoving granite. Standing before it an elderly English socialist told me that in the whole mess of human history *this* at least – the statue and all it stands for – was something of which we could be proud. He said that he had no use for religion, but that he felt he had unknowingly been a follower of the Buddha all along.

An intensely private reflection, its disclosure prompted perhaps by the power of the figure: but what is remarkable is that it should be found in so many others. Here, for example, is the anthropologist Claude Levi-Strauss, by no means a Buddhist, writing in a similar vein:

what have I learnt from the masters I have listened to, the philosophers I have read, the societies I have investigated, and that very science in which the West takes such pride? Simply a fragmentary lesson or two which, if laid end to end, would add up to the meditations of the Sage at the foot of his tree.

This testifies to the fascination the Buddha still holds for us. Is it justified? What does an Oriental seer, born in the middle of the first millennium before Christ among historical circumstances and a culture so different from our own, have to offer such very modern thinkers? This is the first question I have tried to answer.

And I have tried to answer it by writing a biography of the Buddha. That this is a reasonable strategy is by no means obvious, for history is full of figures whose significance lies very little in their personal lives and very much in their teachings alone. But the Buddha is peculiar in this regard, for his teaching and his life are intimately and inextricably mingled.

Let me illustrate this from traditional accounts of the Buddha's life, which have exerted tremendous influence over Buddhists and are now widely available in European languages. The Buddha was born the son of a king, and so grew up with wealth, pleasure and the prospect of power, all goods commonly desired by human beings. As he reached manhood, however, he was confronted with a sick man, an old man and a corpse. He had lived a sheltered life, and these affected him profoundly, for he realised that no wealth or power could prevent him too from experiencing illness, old age and death. He also saw a wandering ascetic, bent on escaping these sufferings. Reflecting on what he had seen, he reached the first great turning-point of his life: against the wishes of his family he renounced home, wife, child and position to become a homeless wanderer, seeking release from this apparently inevitable pain.

For some years he practised the trance-like meditation, and later the strenuous self-mortification, which were then current among such wanderers, but he found these ineffective. So he sat down to reflect quietly, with neither psychic nor physical rigours, on the common human plight. This led to the second great change in his life, for out of this reflection in tranquillity arose at last awakening and release. He had 'done what was to be done', he had solved the enigma of suffering. Deriving his philosophy from his experience he then taught for forty-five years, and his teaching touched most problems in the conduct of human life. He founded an order of monks who were to free themselves by following his example, and they spread his teaching abroad in the world. He eventually died of mortal causes, like others, but unlike others he was 'utterly extinguished' (*parinibbuto*), for he would never be reborn to suffer again.

There are good reasons to doubt even this very compressed account, but at least the outline of the life must be true: birth, maturity, renunciation, search, awakening and liberation, teaching, death. This biography, with the two marked transformations, the renunciation and the awakening, gave the Buddha and his followers the dramatic plot with which to illustrate their belief and the psychological and philosophical model on which to found their thought. Dramatically the action centres on spiritual changes achieved by heroic personal application, while philosophically it centres on discoveries made within the Buddha's own mind and body.

Hence he said, 'it is within this fathom-long carcass, with its mind and its notions, that I declare there is the world, the origin of the world, the cessation of the world and the path leading to the cessation of the world' (S I 62). Within these bounds what he suffered was suffered in common with all mortal beings. For all mortals, in his words, 'birth is suffering, ageing is suffering, sickness is suffering.' In his view these inescapable and pressing facts were discoverable by anyone through introspection into their own experience. Similarly the means of release were available to everyone. The meditation methods which he developed, for example, are based on such simple and available phenomena as one's own breathing. The morality he espoused was founded in clear and practical principles derived from his own life. The Buddha's laboratory was himself, and he generalised his findings to cover all human beings.

So the second question is, how did the Buddha change and develop? For it is this development which is, in one way or another, the subject of his philosophy. It is a question which has been of central concern to Buddhists, and it is one which the Buddha himself frequently answered. Sometimes he answered it directly by recounting part of his life. Elsewhere he answered it indirectly by stating that if one did X, then the following deleterious consequences would ensue, but if one did Y, then the consequences would be wholesome and conducive to liberation. Behind this lay the assumption that the Buddha knew this because he had witnessed the alternatives. He required of himself, as of his monks, adherence to one rule of evidence: 'that which you affirm [must be] that which you have realised, seen, known for yourself' (M I 265).

It does not follow from the autobiographical nature of the Buddha's philosophy, however, that an account of the Buddha alone would be adequate to explain it. For despite his taste for solitude he was part of his society and its history. He lived amid great and decisive social and intellectual changes, changes whose fruits he inherited and to whose further course he contributed substantially. His thought was revolutionary, but it was a revolution which had already been in the making for a long time. The image I have in mind is that of a wave of change which built up slowly, over centuries, touching every aspect of the lives of the ancient Indians. The Buddha was elevated to the crest of this wave, and he enjoyed a wide view across human affairs. The problem is to assess how much of his vision he owed to his elevation, to his position in history and to the work of his predecessors and contemporaries, and how much to the keenness of his own sight.

What evidence do we possess to recount the life and circumstances of a man who lived 2500 years ago? For the life of the Buddha we rely almost entirely on the Buddhist scriptures, preserved in many oriental languages, which have at least the advantage of being very extensive. Those portions which are oldest and which most narrowly concern the Buddha, the *Basket of Discourses* (*Suttapiṭaka*) and the *Basket of the Disciplinary Code* (*Vinayapiṭaka*), take up several library shelves in their various versions. Most of these, furthermore, are represented as being utterances of the Buddha, each spoken on a particular occasion in a particular place. The intention of the Buddha's followers was evidently to preserve the actual words of their teacher in their historical setting.

How well did they achieve this intention? Let us look first at the formation of the Buddhist canon. The canonical discourses take various forms: sometimes they are dialogues into which the Buddha entered with followers of other teachings; sometimes they are answers to specific questions brought to him by his own monks; sometimes they are lessons directed to his monks; and occasionally they are sermons addressed to the laymen who did not leave their homes but were content to support those who did.

The monks were chiefly responsible for preserving this teaching, since it was largely directed to them. The Buddha and his monks were peripatetic for much of the year, but gathered together in separate monasteries for the four months of the rainy season retreat, during the North Indian monsoon. While wandering the Buddha and his monks spread the message abroad, but while in retreat they discussed and rehearsed the teaching. Indeed, a few of the canonical discourses consist of discussions between monks. Throughout the canon are found slightly different versions of some doctrine or other, and this is no doubt partly attributable to elaborations at the hands of the monks, either during the Buddha's lifetime or after his death. But it also seems likely that the Buddha sometimes changed or improved his teachings, and that the dispersal of the monks allowed both earlier and later versions to be preserved among them, each in a different place.

It was after the Buddha's death that the real work of preservation began. The monks probably held a council shortly after that event, and almost certainly another was held a century later. At these councils they made an effort to establish or authenticate the then extant accounts of the life and teaching of the Buddha, and they were aware of systematic rules governing the acceptance or rejection of a discourse as authentic. Moreover the monks brought to the task of preservation a number of devices. They adopted from the culture around them or developed themselves methods of recitation and memorisation. They gave many of the discourses a repetitious and formulaic shape, which facilitated such memorisation. They used poetry, which was probably sung – though the Buddha may have already done this as well. And, most important, they divided the discourses into distinct but largely overlapping bodies of material, each of which became the responsibilities of certain monks to memorise and pass on. The scriptures were not written down until three or four hundred years after the death of the Buddha, but these oral and social methods ensured that his words were probably kept better than our print-bound culture would recognise.

This is not to say that the canonical materials are wholly faithful. Some of the Buddha's words were lost, others misunderstood. Some became formulae which were repeated in inappropriate contexts. Moreover the monks added a good deal themselves, and in particular the figure of the Buddha tended to be magnified. Indeed none of the languages in which the canon now appears was the language of the Buddha himself, whatever it was, though one of them, Pali, is probably very close to it. From internal evidence it seems certain that these oldest texts had crystallised into roughly the shape in which we have them by the time of the second council or shortly thereafter. So at best we can hope to see the Buddha about as well as did his own disciples three generations after his death.

However, it took many Western scholars, working for more than a century, to conclude this much. For some time not too long after the second council the Buddhist order was riven by schisms, and as each group moved apart it preserved the old texts, but rearranged them. And indeed the principle throughout Buddhist history was that, whatever rearrangements occurred, nothing was discarded. But to the old material different schools added new material, and the now expanded canons of each group represented different emphases, and new doctrines, in one or other of the related North Indian languages of Pali, Sanskrit or one of the Prakrits. These ancient developments took place within the Indian subcontinent, and of this period are preserved in an Indian language only the Pali canon in its entirety and some fragments in the other languages.

But much of the other material still exists in translation. For still later, slightly less than a thousand years after the death of the Buddha, Buddhism moved to China, and subsequently to Tibet, and a great deal of the material which has now been lost from Indian languages was translated into Chinese and Tibetan and thereby preserved. In these translated canons, however, the old teachings were now quite surrounded, and in effect obscured, by teachings different from those espoused by the Buddha. The Buddhist world, as Western scholarship found it in the nineteenth century, presented practices and opinions at least as varied among themselves as those among Christian churches.

It at first seemed easy to accept that the Pali canon, preserved by the Theravadins (School of the Elders) of Sri Lanka Burma and Thailand, was the oldest and most genuine. This is what Theravadins themselves claimed. Since then, however, individual scholars have learned the Pali, Sanskrit, Tibetan and Chinese which are required to check such claims, and quite ancient texts have come to light from Central Asian hoards. It now appears that, though the Pali texts are still the single most useful source on the Buddha, in many respects they can be corrected and improved by readings from the Central Asian finds or from Tibetan and Chinese. Certainly the Tibetan and Chinese sources are indispensable for establishing what the oldest sources are. In this book the translations and terms are from the Pali sources, but I have used the conclusions of scholars working in other languages to supplement them.

These texts have many virtues, but they are peculiarly weak on one account, the facts that would make up the Buddha's *Who's Who* entry. Most troublesome is the Buddha's chronology. The scriptures give us license to accept that he lived to a ripe age, eighty years, and that he taught for forty-five years. But the actual dates are another matter. Sources preserved in Sri Lanka and corrected by Western scholars yield a date for the Buddha's death in 483 BC. Sources preserved in Chinese suggest 368 BC. The question is still being actively debated, and will probably go on being debated, for in either case the argument depends upon a long and tenuous chain of inference.

The problem illustrates a trait characteristic of the ancient Indians altogether: that they were very little interested in chronology but much exercised over philosophy. Hence we are in the paradoxical situation of having a better idea of what the Buddha thought than of what century he lived in.

This is not to say, however, that the sources are weak on history. The Buddha was a practical man who often spoke through concrete examples from the life around him, and this reveals a great deal about his world. The monks' efforts to conserve the Buddha's words in a realistic setting have the same effect. We learn about what occupations people pursued, how people classified each other, what kind of political arrangements there were, and what religious institutions were current. It is possible to construct quite a rich and complex picture of the Buddha's India, a picture that can be corroborated from the scriptures of the Buddhists' rivals, the Jains. Indeed it may be said that with the Buddha India first enters history, for in any narrative account it is only at the Buddha's time that detail becomes clear enough to write with confidence of particular kings and states, particular economic arrangements, particular religious teachers and their doctrines.

This relatively static picture can moreover be set in motion by comparison with other sources. For the period preceding the Buddha we have the Sanskrit texts of the Brahmanical tradition (what was later to become Hinduism proper), the *Brahmaṇas* and *Upanishads*. These possess little of the revealing detail of the Buddhist scriptures, since they are the technical literature of a sacrificial, and later an esoteric, cult; nor do they refer to a single period, having been composed over many centuries. But they do testify that the earlier society was quite different in kind from that of the age of the Buddha. These differences are moreover confirmed by the archaeological record. A few centuries before the Buddha there were no cities proper and no states, only a series of small warrior principalities. At the time of the Buddha there were both cities and states, and a century or two after his death North India was to support the Mauryan empire, the greatest state in the subcontinent until the British Raj. The Buddha lived amidst the rise of Indian civilisation, just as Socrates lived amidst the rise of Western civilisation in ancient Greece.

There also developed in ancient India new and enduring habits of thought, which are in some respects so similar to our own that we have difficulty recognising them at all. Here the comparison with ancient Greece is especially helpful, for only by looking back to that period of our own history do we find these habits actually being formed. We now take for granted a language and a way of thinking in which we can talk about human societies in general, or discuss what a universal morality might entail. We are acquainted with the notion that fundamental questions may be asked about ourselves, and that the answers might apply broadly to people in quite different situations. Moreover we easily suppose that such matters can be discussed according to impersonal criteria of truth available to anyone. In sum, we are familiar with thought which is general not particular; abstract not concrete; and argued rather than certified by supernatural sanction, illustrated by customary imagery or sanctioned by tradition.

But when we look to Socrates and his predecessors in Greece, and to the Buddha and his forebears in India, these habits seem fresh and newly acquired. This does not mean that the earlier Greeks or Indians were unable to consider their nature or their society. They certainly did so. But they did so in a way that constrained their reflections within the narrow viewpoint of their own group. They spoke best for themselves and to themselves, and only someone born within the society could fully participate in the fruits of their thought. For their thought was symbolic, in the specific sense that it evoked or expressed – rather than questioned or explained – the shared experience and values of a relatively small-scale community. So long as that experience was shared, and so long as that community did not embrace too many disparate elements, there was no reason, indeed no occasion, for questioning the values.

But with the rise of cities and the growth of a complex, cosmopolitan community, experience was no longer shared nor values unquestioned. The easy correspondence between traditional thought and life no longer held. There were substantial changes in the forms of common life, and with those changes arose the possibility that those forms could be reconsidered, discussed and reasoned over; people could now philosophise about them. This is the import of Cicero's dictum about Socrates, that he 'first called philosophy down from the skies, set it in the cities and even introduced it into homes, and compelled it to consider life and morals, good and evil'. Much the same could be said of the Buddha. Neither was much interested in God, gods or the supernatural, but both were passionately concerned with the ends and the conduct of human life.

2 Early life and renunciation

Later traditions embroidered a great deal on the Buddha's early life and appearance, but of this we can rely on little. The conventional images of him are perhaps true to his characteristic posture in meditation, but since such images were not made until centuries after his death they cannot be portraits. There are some grounds for believing that he was handsome according to the tastes of his time, for a relatively early source, the *Aggañña Sutta*, praises his beauty at the expense of the neighbouring king Pasenadi. As for his character apart from his philosophy, little can be said, for in our sources his character *is* his philosophy. We might justifiably assume, however, that he was passionately intense and rebellious in his youth, for no placid and obedient character could have set out to do what he did, still less achieve it.

We are on firmer ground with two facts. First, the Buddha was born among the Sakya people, probably at their capital, Kapilavatthu, now the town of Lumbini in the lowland Terai region of Nepal. Second, his family or clan name was Gotama (Sanskrit *Gautama*; he was not called Buddha, 'awakened', until after the awakening, but for convenience I will use the title throughout). These facts reveal nothing about his childhood or education, but they do place him in the wider Gangetic civilisation of which he was a part, and they suggest something of the circumstances which he inherited.

The Sakyas were one of a number of peoples spread along the northern edge of the Ganges basin, at the periphery of the then developing North Indian civilisation. When the Buddha was born these peoples were still more or less independent and had roughly similar systems of government. They were ruled by oligarchies or councils of elders, or some mixture of the two, and might therefore best be called tribal republics. Some of these might have elected a leader for a fixed term, but they did not have kings in the strict sense, and therefore the later tradition that the Buddha was a king's son must be dismissed. However the Sakyas considered themselves to have the effective rank of kings, nobles, and warriors in respect of the wider civilisation, and indeed they probably did not recognise, as others did, the ceremonial precedence of Brahmans, priests of high rank. They considered themselves an élite, and it is difficult to resist the impression that the Buddha had the confidence of high birth in his dealings with the wider world.

There is evidence that the Sakyans struggled to remain aloof from that world, but they were already deeply embroiled in it. The Buddha's clan name, Gotama, was itself used elsewhere, and probably originally, by Brahmans. Indeed the very scale against which the Sakyans claimed their high status really only made sense beyond their borders. Moreover they were already in effect tributaries to a king in the south, and were probably tied economically to southern commerce. The Sakyans, and the tribal republics as a whole, were more acted upon than acting. They were to contribute to Indian civilisation only their great kinsman, the Buddha, and certain of their values preserved in his teaching.

The centres of change, and of power, lay in the central Ganges basin. A collection of small heroic warrior societies had spread along the river centuries earlier, and these societies developed into centralised monarchical states. There was a traditional list of sixteen of these 'great countries', but already in the Buddha's youth some had swallowed others and were on the way to further conquests. One, Kosala, conquered the Sakyas in the Buddha's lifetime. Another, Magadha, already ruler of western Bengal and destined to be the nucleus of the Mauryan empire, was to engulf the Vajji confederacy of tribal republics after his death. The future lay with the kings, and not with the republics.

At the heart of these states appeared true urban centres where there had been none before. These swelling cities contained the kings' courts, and to the courts and cities were drawn the makings of an urban life: merchants and craftsmen with new skills, soldiers and labourers, conquered lords to render tribute, the displaced, the foreigners, the opportunists. There was a more complex division of labour and of status between people, and those of different languages and cultures were now thrown together to get along as best they could. The court and the city also drew the countryside into relation with this urban life, through force wielded by the king's soldiers and officials, through the subtler effect of long-distance commerce and through movements of population. The archaeological record shows no planning in these ancient Indian cities: they were chaotic, and that chaos perhaps best symbolises both the difficulties and the creative possibilities of these newly complex societies. Above all the question was, how were the Indians to understand themselves among these unprecedented forms of common life?

They began with one very old intellectual tool, a conception of the different estates in society. This was the property of the old heroic warrior societies, and is reminiscent of the medieval European division of society into those who pray, those who fight and those who labour: Church, nobility and peasants. In the Indian case there were four estates (Sanskrit *varṇa*). At the top were the Brahmans, priests of the sacrificial religion and intellectuals. Despite their rank, however, they did not wield power. That was left to the second estate, the Warriors (*khattiya*, Sanskrit *kṣatriya*), whose duty it was to fight, to rule and to pay for sacrifice. This is the rank claimed by the Sakyans, and into this category fell kings and nobility. The third estate were the commoners, the producers, Husbandmen (Sanskrit *vaiśya*). And the fourth estate were the Servants (Sanskrit *śudra*), those ineligible for the benefits of sacrificial religion and compelled to a life of servitude under the other three orders. This conception *prescribed* an orderly and hierarchical relationship between the estates, each having certain claims on the others and certain obligations towards them, and each owing respect to the ones above. It also more or less *described* society, for these were communities of rank in which a warrior élite, with their priests, ruled over commoners and the still lower populace of the conquered.

But, most important, this conception of estates was a deeply held and pervasive way of looking at the human world. It was not merely an ideology of different occupations or social ranks, for it also purported to describe the essential characteristics of the people in each estate. To call someone a Warrior, for example, was not just to designate him as a bearer of arms and a ruler, but also to say that he was rich, powerful, generous, heroic and of noble birth. A Brahman was not just a priest by function, but also inherently endowed with wisdom, virtue, learning, personal purity and purity of birth. And to call someone a Servant was not merely to refer to his job, but also to his poverty, weakness, vileness and low birth. Everything significant that was to be known about a person was known through his estate, whether for religious, psychological, political, economic or social purposes. A person's appearance, psychic and physical endowments, his very essence was determined by his estate. It was as if the estates were different species. In this conception there were no human beings, only Brahmans, Warriors, Husbandmen and Servants; rather as in the theory of apartheid there are only Blacks, Whites and Coloureds. In the texts of the older warrior societies, the *Brahmaṇas*, this order of estates is wholly taken for granted. It arose from the experience of the pre-urban Gangetic Indians and expressed the nature of their society. If it was unfair from our point of view, that unfairness was already built into their world in many ways.

However, the estates theory did not bear the same intimate and organic connection to the world centred upon the cities as it had to the earlier heroic world, and that for several reasons. First, it did not comprehend the new variety and complexity of occupation and position. In the older texts, for example, we read nothing of merchants; but in the Buddhist and Jain texts they are a very visible and active part of the scene. In the older texts there are only Warriors, but in the newer there are paid soldiers and salaried officials as well. These and other specialisations were dependent upon the new states and the use of money, which arrived in North India only with the cities. These new categories of persons presented the estates theory with formidable difficulties. The theory envisaged a simple agrarian and pastoral world inhabited by four kinds of people. Where did these new figures fit in? What sort of persons were they?

But that was by no means the most pressing challenge offered by the new circumstances, for there was another which struck at the very heart of the estates. This is adumbrated in a Buddhist discourse (M II no. 84) which makes two relevant points. First, it asserts that a criminal, whether Brahman or Servant, Warrior or Husbandman, would be sentenced by the king of a newly centralised state strictly according to the seriousness of his deed, not according to his estate. This was quite contrary to the old view, however, for there the punishment – envisaged as reparation or penance – was to be appropriate to the person, to the estate of the transgressor,

not only to the crime. Were Brahmans and Warriors to be
treated like common criminals? Were the estates not to be res-
pected? And second, the discourse points out that, in the
urbanizing world of the Buddha, it was quite possible for someone born of high estate, a Brahman or a Warrior, to be employed
as a servant by someone of low estate, a Servant or a Husbandman. Such an eventuality was wholly inconceivable under the
old order: Servants could only serve, Brahmans and Warriors
only command.

In the discourse these observations are meant to reveal the
real state of the world, as opposed to the hollow pretensions of
the Brahmans, the upholders of the estates theory. And it is
plausible. If we compare the pre-Buddhist texts with another
new literature which began to appear at about the Buddha's
time, the *Dharmaśastra* (Science of Law; I refer to the earliest,
the *Gautama Dharmaśastra*), we learn that kings were indeed
taking new powers of judgment and punishment. In any case
they could depose old élites, as in the tribal republics, and raise
new ones. We also read in both Buddhist sources and the Law
literature that new financial arrangements – credit and debt,
interest, a market in land – had come into existence. This
bore the possibility that a person of rank and wealth could lose
everything through rapacious business practices, or that a
person of low status could rise by the same means.

The difficulty for the estates theory was that it had described
four ideal types of persons, and each type had been a harmonious blend of characteristics. A Warrior, for example, was a
Warrior by birth, a Warrior by political power, and – since
power was power over people and land, the only sources of
wealth – a Warrior by wealth. But now this was too evidently
contradicted by facts. There were Warriors by birth who had
neither power nor wealth. There were wealthy men, merchants, who had neither birth nor power. And there were

17

powerful men in the new states who were not Warriors by birth. A person in any of these positions could have found his actual plight at painful variance with the one attributed to him in the estates scheme. That old version of human nature and the human world simply did not express the new reality.

To this problem there were two responses. The first was that of the Brahmans, the theorists of the estates. In their Science of Law, a series of texts which appeared over many centuries after the Buddha, they gradually amended that theory. Their strategy, as in so much of Indian thought, was to keep the old but to build on new additions. They retained the hierarchical order of the estates simply by putting new occupations in old slots: merchants were placed with Husbandmen, while many craft specialities were put in the Servant estate. Regional groups or tribes were distributed among the lower three estates. They also devised a theory to explain the appearance of hereditary local or occupational groups – now called castes – as the result of intermarriage between different estates. In this enterprise they were, in the long run, so successful that Indians today still understand the complex order of castes according to the simple estates scheme.

But our interest lies with the other response. This was formed, quite in opposition to the Brahmans, by the ascetics and philosophical wanderers whose ranks the Buddha was to join. Their answer is found in both Buddhist and Jain sources, and it is so fundamental to the ascetics' point of view that it must have been already present, in rough form at least, when the Buddha arrived on the scene.

The Buddha expressed this common view in an especially clear form in dialogue with a Brahman (D I no. 4). In the dialogue he asks the Brahman the leading question, 'what makes a true Brahman?' This in effect amounts to asking, 'what makes the best, the supreme species of humankind?', for according to the estates scheme the Brahman is just that. In reply the Brahman claims that he and his fellows hold their elevated position by virtue of a number of qualities which they enjoy simultaneously. They are at once of highest birth, of greatest learning, the most beautiful, the wisest and the most virtuous.

This is perfectly orthodox: the Brahman believes himself to be an harmonious bundle of praiseworthy qualities. But then the Buddha dissects this claim by enquiring into its details. Could one fairly claim to be a Brahman without pure descent through seven generations on both sides? Well, apparently so. Could one claim to be a Brahman without mastery of Brahmanical learning? Yes. Could one claim to be a Brahman without physical beauty? Most assuredly. But could one claim Brahman status without wisdom and without virtue? No, replied the Brahman, for these were the very grounds on which Brahmans stood, the foundation of their claim to spiritual leadership and high rank.

Wisdom and virtue. One doubts that a Brahman could really have been forced to make these damning admissions, but the very fact that an argument of this form could be made points to a substantial change in intellectual climate. For now not only was the Brahmanical view challenged, but also those two qualities, wisdom and virtue, had become detached from traditional Brahmanical interpretations of them. Virtue: now there was some general view of what might constitute good behaviour quite apart from what might be appropriate to a particular estate. For the Buddha's point is that virtue is something anyone can have: it is not ascribed by birth, but achieved by application. And likewise wisdom is to be achieved and cannot just be ascribed. So the true Brahman is simply the person, born of whatever parentage, who has both wisdom and virtue.

The argument is directed against Brahman pretensions and

favours the ascetics' claims to possess wisdom and virtue. But the implication is far greater, for it implies that there is some basic human nature, capable of wisdom and virtue, quite apart from one's estate or position. At a stroke the bewildering variety of different ranks and different fates was set in the background, while in the foreground was set one simple common endowment. In principle any human being can become wise and good. This assumption was made, in one way or another, by many of the Buddha's contemporaries. They spoke, not merely to this or that condition, to this or that estate, but to the human condition as such. It was a revolutionary step, for until it was taken the Indians had no way of speaking of human life beyond the narrow local conception of estates, bound to the older order of Indian society. They now had the opportunity to speak to a very much wider world, and it was an opportunity that the Buddha exploited more than any of his fellows.

*

This may seem momentous to us, but in fact it was but a small part of a much greater project which the Buddha inherited from the wanderers when he renounced the world. Their concern was not so much human society as its horizons: birth and death, and the vast spiritual cosmos which lay behind the fleeting appearances of this life. They looked upon the society of the Ganges basin as though from afar, and disdained it. They were indeed homeless wanderers (*paribbajakas*), spiritual strivers (*samaṇas*), renouncers of the world and all its fruits. But they were also perhaps India's only true cosmopolitans, citizens of the whole, not just of part.

Their cosmopolitanism is shown by the fact that the young Buddha-to-be knew enough of them in his provincial home to decide to join them. The earliest sources on his renunciation are bare and simple, but they attest well enough to the perspective of the renouncers. He was just 'a youth, with coal-black hair, in the early stages of life' (M I 163) when he left the world. This casts doubt on the existence of the wife and child later traditions awarded him, but it does illustrate that to leave the world was a whole life's vocation.

There was also a specific motive for renunciation: 'it occurred to me that life in the home is cramped and dirty, while the life gone forth into homelessness is wide open; it is difficult to live a spiritual life completely perfect and pure in all its parts while cabinned inside' (M I 241). From this we can infer some of the adventurous high-mindedness associated with the wanderer's life in the Buddha's time. They sought an ideal of perfection elevated beyond the squalid exigencies and mean quarrels of ordinary experience. They were bent not on their own pleasure, but on a lofty enterprise which sometimes brought them honour but also struggle and difficulty. To be a renouncer was a young man's, indeed a romantic's, aspiration, and from this point of view the Buddha was but one of many youths who left home, attracted by the challenge of the wandering life.

But the counterpart to this enthusiasm was a sombre and deeply serious view of such a life's task. First, the refined ideals of virtue and wisdom laid upon these wanderers a burden of perfection which perhaps few could achieve in detail. And second, they left ordinary life not just because of its irritations, but also because of its dangers. In the bare account of his reflections before renunciation the Buddha's first great change of heart is described thus:

Why, since I am myself subject to birth, ageing, disease, death, sorrow and defilement, do I seek after what is also subject to these things? Suppose, being myself subject to these things, seeing danger in them, I were to seek the unborn, unageing, undiseased, deathless, sorrowless, undefiled supreme surcease of bondage, the extinction of all these troubles?

This account is filtered through the Buddha's later thought, but what we can see through the filter is the starkness of the alternatives. The unexamined and uncontrolled life of the home leads only to sorrow and despair, endlessly repeated. Only the renouncer's life offers hope, the hope of looking down upon a morass of desire and suffering from an eminence of knowledge and dispassion. Western writers have often counted this view as unrelieved pessimism, but they have missed the optimism, the prospect of attaining 'the deathless'. The renouncers' attitude was compounded of dark bitterness and bright hope.

What rendered this attitude compelling was a larger theory which lay behind it, explaining and justifying the renouncers' rejection of the world. In this view the ordinary activity of the householder was contrasted with the extraordinary inactivity of the renouncer. For the householder must commit acts or deeds (Sanskrit *karman*) in pursuit of his worldly ends such as sexual pleasure, procreation, the acquisition of goods and power over others. Such deeds do not include inconsequential ones such as, say, brushing your teeth, but only those which are consequential or fruitful, which substantially affect your own or someone else's condition. Moreover these deeds have spiritual consequences beyond the purely visible ones, for they are charged with the power to create another body and life for the hapless householder, causing him to be reborn. (If this seems peculiar it should be remembered that it is no less rational than the belief that our deeds consign us to heaven or hell, or that they call down on us supernatural retribution.) And in being reborn he is condemned to suffer and desire in another life just as he does in this one. The suffering of one life, therefore, is but a sample of the endless suffering one will inevitably experience as one dies and is reborn again and again in the 'running on and on', *saṃsāra*, of life in the world, of desire and sorrow.

In contrast the renouncer lives in celibacy, poverty, harmlessness and desirelessness, which amount not so much to good activity as to inactivity, for he simply does not commit acts which are charged with the awful power to cause him to be reborn. Thereby the successful renouncer escapes the cycle of rebirth completely. True, the householder may achieve a better rebirth (in heaven or as a Brahman) by good deeds, or a worse one (in hell or as an animal) by bad deeds. The householder can control his fate to this extent. But this is as nothing beside the fact that, in whatever birth, even the most exalted, suffering, death and rebirth are inevitable. Only by renouncing the world entirely, by giving up all flawed activity, can one escape from this awesome mechanism into the 'unborn, unageing, undiseased, and deathless'.

This law of causation is impersonal, not administered by a god, and universal, for it applies to all sentient beings, animal, human or supernatural, who are reborn in accordance with their acts. Certainly it must have been the development of this view, and not just a criticism of the estate theory, which led the renouncers to discover human nature. For the Buddhist discourse which remarks that anyone can become a servant or that anyone is punished by a king according to his deeds, also appeals to this universal law of causation. Everyone, the discourse says, whether Brahman or Servant, must experience the consequences of his deeds in another life, but anyone, Brahman or Servant, may become a renouncer to escape rebirth entirely. These are the fundamental refutations of the estate theory: the social criticism was incidental. What the renouncers saw was the plight of all sentient beings, among whom the human condition was but a special case.

As a novice the Buddha must have found this clearer in outline than in its details. But in any case both the theory of moral causation and the project of escaping it were already established, though on the scale of centuries it was relatively new. In the older pre-Buddhist texts there are only a few hints of it. In later pre-Buddhist texts, the *Upanishads*, it had taken shape. And by the Buddha's time reincarnation was commonly accepted and the renouncers had become in effect a fifth estate, a notably important part of the life of society. There are many unanswered, and unanswerable, questions about how the renouncers and their world-view developed, but in any case their practices and their theory must have developed together. Only a body of men whose practices were moving away from ordinary life could have come to adopt such a distant and sombre view, and only such a grand, general, and all-embracing theory could have justified such a hard life or inspired people throughout the Ganges basin to respect and support the renouncers as mendicants.

The renouncers were made by their world, but they also made it, as teachers, preachers and exemplars. Their theory of reincarnation has frequently been treated as an irrational religious view, perhaps even a very old one which was already present when the warrior societies conquered North India. There may be some truth in this, but it ignores the power of the theory to explain a complex world, as it ignores the theory's relative sophistication. Whether one were favourably endowed by birth or not, whether one were rising in the king's court or had lost one's ancestral lands, whether one were successful in business or were defeated by the king's armies, the theory could explain it. Success, beauty and power in this world are the result of good acts in a previous life. The humble goodness of the poor now will garner its just reward in the next life, while prosperous wrongdoing will be punished. Moreover, not only events within life, but its ultimate ends — birth, old age and death — were set within a much larger scheme within which they could be remedied. It is not at all surprising that the theory was accepted so widely, in one form or another, throughout Indian civilisation, and even by Brahmans. In its use of abstract moral categories of good and evil to apply to all acts, in its positing of a natural law of cause and effect, and in its impersonality it was the product of generations or centuries of intellectual effort. It would continue to be refined and developed by the Buddha and his contemporaries.

*

In the earlier Brahmanical texts the discussion and debate which led to these developments is relatively muted or even silent; but in the Buddhist and Jain texts which reveal the Buddha's immediate environment a multitude of contending voices speak, as though in a tumultuous market-place of philosophical opinions and ascetic practices. There were indeed public debating halls where ascetics of all stamps gathered to dispute. The public lecture or sermon, directed to disciples but also to potential lay supporters, was a common institution. Certain practices were shared – begging, wandering, celibacy, self-restraint – but upon this basic fabric were embroidered a welter of different opinions and philosophies and a fantastic variety of inventive self-torments.

There was an element of self-display in this. Some ate like dogs, others adopted the posture of a chicken, many went naked. More important, much of the self-display was intellectual: the Buddha was later to inveigh against those who were 'clever, subtle, experienced in controversy, hairsplitters who writhe like worms in argument'. But the very terms of abuse put in the mouths of such 'hairsplitters' demonstrate a heightened quality of debate and the spread of those habits of mind which would allow people to decide between one argument and another: 'you conclude with your assumptions, you assume your conclusions'; 'work to clarify your views';

25

'disentangle yourself if you can'. There were different schools of sceptics, philosophers doubtful of the possibility of effective knowledge in this or that matter, and their existence was perhaps the surest sign of the heat and sophistication of the intellectual climate. There were materialists who wholly denied the existence of that unseen spiritual cosmos of transmigration. There were predestinarians who believed in transmigration but who felt that every sentient being must pass through every possible fate before release was possible.

Most relevant to the Buddha, however, are three movements, the first of which can be traced through the Brahmanical texts. In the oldest sacrificial literature the sacrifice had been directed to the person of the sacrificer, in his bodily parts and faculties, in order to imbue him with magical power for the this-worldly ends of success, fertility and long life. This evolved towards a concern with the other world, life after death, and simultaneously towards a more inward conception of the sacrificer's person, now his Self. And in the *Upanishads*, composed perhaps not long before the time of the Buddha, it is the Self, the inner essence, which is the subject of transmigration, travelling from birth to birth.

The second movement was that of yoga, which in the relevant aspects was so similar to the Upanishadic movement that we may fairly speak of a spectrum of yogic/Upanishadic doctrines. Through the Buddhist scriptures which attack these yogic/Upanishadic views we glimpse a wealth of speculation and many finely differentiated teachings proposing various views of the Self: some said that it was material, some that it was fine-material or made of mind only, while yet others held that each individual has several increasingly refined Selves. With each view went a slightly different construction of the spiritual cosmos and a panoply of meditation techniques aimed at attaining this Self so that one could sink into it, beyond the pain and confusion of the world and of transmigration.

The third movement is one which we associate today most closely with Jainism. The founder of Jainism was Mahāvīra, a contemporary of the Buddha; but there is ample evidence that his teaching was largely given in doctrines already in existence, and these doctrines enjoyed a wide influence. This school held a particularly strong version of the transmigration theory, to the effect that to hurt any living being, each of which has a soul, is to injure one's own soul by making defilement adhere to it, as dirt to a cloth. In order to cleanse oneself of defilement already acquired one was to undertake voluntary self-mortification such as fasting; and to avoid further defilement one was to avoid any injury to living beings, great or small: this is the doctrine of harmlessness or non-violence, *ahimsa*. Jain self-mortification blended on one extreme with the self-restraint generally expected of all renouncers, and on the other with self-torments of a quite spectacular kind. And similarly harmlessness or non-violence was a common part of the renouncer's morality, practised perhaps most enthusiastically by Jains and proto-Jains but found among others as well.

The Buddha's relation to these movements was complex. In the first place he took some of their offerings and rejected others. He built upon the yogic/Upanishadic concern with introspection and he developed their meditative techniques, but he rejected the yogis' doctrines of the Self. He adapted the teaching of harmlessness to his own purposes, but he discarded self-mortification. However, it was never just a matter of borrowing what he found plausible or of being passively influenced by his predecessors and contemporaries, for what he did accept he transformed, and what he rejected he rejected for reasons which were original and creative. The Buddha found himself in a vigorous, competitive world which importuned him on all sides with predatory demands for total intellectual allegiance and total acceptance of one way of life or another. The relative simplicity and the cool, magisterial tone of the Buddha's teaching disguise the intensity of his struggle to find his own voice among so many others.

3 To the awakening

When the Buddha left home he walked south towards the centres of population strung out along the central Ganges basin, and until his death he continued to wander throughout an area roughly 250 miles long and 150 miles wide, from Kosambi in the west to Campā in the east. There does exist a late and unreliable chronology of much of this period, but more to the point is the pattern of the Buddha's wandering life. He evidently spent time in the depths of the forest, and even sheltered in a cowshed. He had contact with both kings and prostitutes, merchants and Brahmans. His role as a peripatetic mendicant allowed him a freedom to see every way of life and every corner of his civilisation. He enjoyed a licence allowed to those, the religious beggars, who belonged to no particular part of society, free to move everywhere because in principle they threatened no one. Perhaps only a merchant or a pedlar – those other figures so characteristic of the Buddha's civilisation – would have seen so much of that world, would have had such a cosmopolitan experience.

But though the Buddha witnessed his world comprehensively, he was not of it. He was set apart by the high-minded personal morality of the renouncers: 'as a lotus flower is born in water, grows in water, and rises out of water to stand above it unsoiled, so I, born in the world, raised in the world, having overcome the world, live unsoiled by the world' (A II 38–9). He sometimes shared a roof with other wanderers, and stayed frequently for long periods of time in forested parks near the great cities – Rājagaha, Sāvatthi, Benares, Vesāli, Kosambi –

which were reserved for wanderers or, later, for the growing Buddhist order.

What we know of this formative period of the Buddha's life, of his encounters with the other wanderers, is contained in a brief, bare account which, shorn of its repetitions and untrustworthy detail, would occupy but a page or two in translation: no very promising source for biography. However, this narrative is cast in terms which themselves can be glossed in considerable detail from other, doctrinal discourses of the Buddha, and once the narrative is unpacked in this way it becomes a more fruitful source than it first appears. To the keen sceptical scholarly eye there is no single detail of the narrative that could pass unquestioned; but the story as a whole is so well connected with the rest of the Buddha's teaching that it must bear a substantial burden of truth.

In that narrative (M I 163–6) the Buddha's first contacts among the renouncers are represented as having been with two teachers of yogic meditation, Āḷāra Kālāma and Uddaka Rāmaputta. The Buddha went first to Āḷāra Kālāma, and 'in no long time' mastered his teaching 'as far as lip reciting and repetition went'. Realising that this doctrine – itself significantly left undescribed in the narrative – was founded in the teacher's meditative experience, the Buddha asked him, 'To what extent do you declare you have attained this doctrine, witnessing it directly through meditative knowledge?' Āḷāra Kālāma replied that he had attained it as far as the Meditative Plane of nothingness. The Buddha then achieved this meditative state, and when he returned to describe his accomplishment to Āḷāra Kālāma, the latter was so pleased that he invited the Buddha to become his fellow teacher and leader. But the Buddha reflected that 'this teaching does not lead to dispassion, to the fading of desire, to cessation, to peace, to direct knowledge in meditation, to awakening, to release; it leads only to the Meditative Plane of nothingness'. He therefore left Āḷāra Kālāma and went to Uddaka Rāmaputta, where the same course of events took place, the only difference being that Uddaka Rāmaputta's teaching was found to lead, not to awakening, but only to the Meditative Plane of neither perception nor non-perception, so the Buddha left him as well.

This was in some ways the most important chapter of the Buddha's search, and clearly any understanding of its significance must turn on the Meditative Planes. What were they? And why did the Buddha reject them?

The fundamental practice used to attain such states is roughly similar in all Indian meditative systems, whether the Buddhist or the yogic/Upanishadic. One begins by sitting cross-legged with a straight back in some quiet place. The straightness of the back and the folded legs foster a degree of wakefulness which could not be obtained in a more comfortable position, such as lying down. One then concentrates on some object, in some versions at first a physical object but eventually in almost every case a mental image, a single sensation, or perhaps a silently repeated sound. In an Upanishadic version one might perhaps have concentrated on the Self dwelling in the heart, 'smaller than a mustard seed and golden' (C III 14). Or in a Buddhist version one might concentrate upon a colour such as blue; or in both a Buddhist and a yogic meditation on one's own breath. The counterpart to this concentration on one object is the strenuous exclusion from the attention of other sensations and indeed of merely adventitious thoughts. One is thereby absorbed in the object of meditation – and indeed some measure of this absorption is experienced by anyone who concentrates on some task.

But because the object is held unchanging before the mind's

eye for long periods of time, quite extraordinary effects are achieved. Psychologists who have investigated such effects confirm not only that measurable physical changes accompany such meditation, but also that – quite apart from beliefs about what should happen – there are psychological changes such as a heightened awareness of the object of meditation, feelings of comfort and pleasure, and detachment from the surroundings and from one's own preoccupations. (These states are now much better known in the West than they were a generation ago.)

On the scale of meditative accomplishments these are relatively modest effects. There are others as well, such as the appearance of peculiar sensations or a light; and even entire complex visions may be witnessed. These further effects may, in some systems, become objects of meditation themselves and may represent the whole purpose of the discipline.

Since all meditative experiences are so radically subjective it seems difficult to find a language in which to couch an objective or value-free account of them. But there are nevertheless circumstantial accounts of a series of meditative states found in Buddhist texts, states which correspond roughly to those described in some yogic texts; and this Buddhist scheme has the advantage from our point of view of offering relatively unadorned descriptions of attitudes and experiences in meditation, descriptions which could as easily describe meditation in one system as in another. Indeed this Buddhist scheme is so untainted by dogma that it has been adopted by Western psychologists attempting to describe the phenomenon of meditation in general.

This scheme is that of the four Absorptions (*jhāna*), a graduated series of increasingly deep meditative states. In the first Absorption the meditator becomes oblivious to everything around him, though still capable of both casual and concerted thought, and his attention dwells unbrokenly on the object of meditation. In this state he enjoys both bodily comfort and the more refined mental pleasure attendant on such relaxed concentration. The meditator in this frame of mind is untroubled by unachieved desires, or by anger, or by torpor, or by doubt and restlessness.

In the second and third Absorptions the meditator gradually leaves off thinking entirely, becoming more and more absorbed in the object of meditation alone, and with this increased concentration and simplification he also transcends his feelings of comfort and intellectual pleasure. He is bent upon the object of meditation alone. And finally, in the fourth Absorption, the meditator is aware only of the object, and of an abiding sense of firm equanimity, beyond feelings of pain or pleasure. Indeed from his point of view he might be said to have increasingly *become* the object of meditation, in that he is aware of little else save the bare fact of his firm concentration or 'one-pointedness'. These four Absorptions were eventually to play a special part in the system of training elaborated by the Buddha, representing specific useful skills in the manipulation of one's own experience.

Beyond the Absorptions, however, there were further meditative accomplishments, the Meditative Planes (*āyatana*). These are described in the Buddhist literature in a relatively abstract and colourless way, but it is very likely that in the yogic systems where they originated they were actually held to be, in some sense, places or spheres, locations in the unseen spiritual cosmos. To reach them was perhaps even conceived as a sort of astral travel. There are hints of such regions in the spiritual cosmography of the *Upanishads* and yogic texts, and the Buddhist descriptions of other yogic systems suggest this as well. Indeed in later Buddhist cosmography these were spiritual planes inhabited by gods. Even the abstract early Buddhist account of them cannot disguise that they are not, like the Absorptions, a general description of meditation appropriate to any number of specific meditation theories, objectives and techniques. They are rather bound to some specific view of the topography of the unseen world. And this is not surprising, for once having resolutely set aside the world of everyday experience such a meditator was likely to supply himself with a map of the territory he had now entered.

In the Buddhist scheme of the Meditative Planes these states are achieved by leaving off 'perceptions of variety', a phrase which, though not entirely clear, seems to mean that the particular qualities perceived in the object of meditation are transcended, so that the meditator remains conscious though no longer with a detailed and defined object of consciousness. And we can see this in the first such state, the 'Meditative Plane of undelimited space'. Here the meditator is conscious of extension, though with no perception of a limitation or a quality in that extension. It is in effect infinite. In the second Meditative Plane, that of 'undelimited consciousness', the meditator is aware of consciousness alone, though with no awareness of a delimiting object of consciousness. In the third Meditative Plane the meditator is barely aware that 'there is nothing' – an awareness, according to more detailed later Buddhist texts, rather like that of coming into a room and finding no one there: it is not an awareness of *who* is not there, but just an awareness of absence. This is the Meditative Plane of nothingness. It can only be transcended in the Meditative Plane of neither perception nor non-perception, in which consciousness is so refined, or suppressed, that the meditator can only just retrieve from such a state an awareness of its existence.

I suspect that such deep trances may account for some of the more spectacular feats of yogic athleticism attested in India today. Breathing is almost wholly suppressed, the heart rate markedly slowed, and other physiological signs yet further altered. Of course this modern Western physiological description was not how the yogis viewed the matter, nor can they have seen it with quite the colourless abstraction of the Buddhist description. In their eyes such experience, being after all the consummation of their efforts, was located in some more highly coloured spiritual landscape. It may have been something like that found in the *Upanishads*, where there is considerable concern with the Self as found in deep sleep, which might have been thought to be equivalent to such profound meditation. Or it may have been like the 'meditation without qualities' found in some early yogic texts of the Indian epic, the *Mahabharata*. But in any case the achievement of such states must be regarded as a testimony to human self-discipline and self-transcendence.

Yet the Buddha rejected such states; or, to be more accurate, he rejected the yogic teachers' assertions that they represented the culmination of the spiritual life. Why? A first approximation to an answer can be found in the *Sallekha Sutta* (M I 40–6), the Discourse on Complete Expunging. There the Buddha outlines the meditative states, both the Absorptions and the Meditative Planes, and he refers to all these as 'tranquil abidings' and as 'comfortable abidings in the here and now'. But these are distinguished from 'complete expunging', i.e. total release from the sufferings of birth and death, which is achieved by following the elaborated path that the Buddha promulgated after his awakening. From this point of view the meditative states are finally inadequate for two reasons. First, they are *merely* temporary states, *only* abidings in the here and now. This criticism is echoed more clearly elsewhere (M III 243–5), where the Buddha notes that, though the skilled meditator can remain for a very long period of time in a meditative state, that state is nevertheless impermanent, liable eventually to dissolve. And again (M III 236–7), a meditator who believes himself to have achieved final and decisive relief through such states is in fact doing something quite different: he is in fact scurrying back and forth pointlessly between 'distress' (ordinary consciousness) and 'the physical comfort of solitude', or at best between 'the fleshless pleasure [of meditation]' and 'the [mere] feeling of neither pleasure nor pain'. So in other words, though these meditative accomplishments offer temporary, even quite long-standing, release, they do not offer a decisive and permanent end to suffering. One must finally emerge only to find that one is still unchanged.

Second, as is implicit in the Discourse on Complete Expunging, such meditative skills are, when compared to the rounded fullness of the Buddha's post-awakening system of training, one-dimensional and narrow, leaving untouched both intellectual and moral development. We can see how this might be so from an analogy with mountain climbing: though the abilities and mental traits developed in such an enterprise might be conducive to some wider development of character in the climber, they do not necessarily do so. Courage and endurance can be used to quite immoral and destructive ends. So though the Buddha had mastered the meditative skills, they did not in themselves release him from ordinary waking life.

It is important, however, to gain a balanced view of what the Buddha was rejecting. On the one hand, he rejected the yogic teachers' claims that their particular accomplishments led to final release. But on the other hand, he implicitly accepted that meditation is, in some ways, the spiritual tool *par excellence*. The Absorptions in particular appear throughout his discourses as accomplishments of great usefulness. A meditator thus skilled would have great powers of concentration; for him there would 'remain an equanimity, cleansed and purified, soft, malleable, and resplendent' (M III 243), like the gold melted and purified by a goldsmith before it is fashioned into an ornament. This concentrated equanimity – of course by no means the sole property of Buddhist meditators – could then be used to attain the final goal of specifically Buddhist awakening and release.

His final view of the Meditative Planes is more difficult to pin down. On the one hand they are sometimes mentioned, in passages sprinkled through the canon, as achievements very near to final release. One could indeed take them a step further to 'complete cessation of what is perceived or felt' by a little more of the same kind of effort. But broadly speaking the canon makes it clear that this 'complete cessation' is not yet final liberation, for beyond that is still required an intellectual and emotional change, the acquisition of a Buddhist wisdom. The Buddha was evidently willing to accept many paths to release, even ones very near those of his yogic teachers; but the final goal still had to be achieved by a quite different step, a change in quality of thought and feeling, not in quantity of meditative effort.

*

The usefulness of the narrative of the Buddha's encounter with the yogis does not end there, however, for it also points to the positive and creative direction the Buddha was to take. This is implicit in the terms in which the yogis are criticised: for it is not their theories which the Buddha here finds wanting – though theories such as they must have held are attacked in many places in his discourses – but their practice. They fall short because, whatever view of the spiritual cosmos clothed their meditative techniques, it was the techniques themselves which were inadequate. On the one hand this signals that the Buddha was to move towards creating his own special forms of meditation, forms beside which methods such as the Absorptions were to take a subsidiary place. On the other hand it betokens the formation of an abiding attitude which must have marked the man as it deeply marked his teaching, an attitude which might be called a stubbornly disciplined pragmatism. Whatever teachings or practices the well-stocked market-place of ancient Indian thought offered him, they had to be shown to be useful in his own experience for him to accept them.

We can understand the significance of this attitude by looking at the Buddha's milieu. Centuries later, India recognised certain authorities or criteria of valid knowledge, by which spiritual truth could be tested, and these criteria were already implicitly present at the Buddha's time. One such criterion was simply whether a teaching appeared in the Brahmanical scriptures, including the *Upanishads*; and we can see that the Buddha was not inclined to accept this, in his view, pretentious and foreign tradition. A second authority the Buddha showed no sign of accepting was the testimony of august inspired teachers of the past on the basis of their supernormal experience. For the Buddha was self-confident, even rebellious, sure that if the problem of suffering were to be solved it had to be of such a nature that he could solve it; and in any case these teachers were not separated from him by centuries in which their knowledge could have gained an unassailable superhuman authority, but were present to him in the flesh and insistent that he could himself experience their knowledge and the liberating fruit of that knowledge. A third authority, that of sheer reasoning or inference, was hardly amenable to him, perhaps because of his already formed commitment to meditation. So he depended wholly upon a fourth criterion, that of direct personal knowledge, direct personal experience, 'direct witnessing in the here and now'. As the Buddha expresses it this criterion seems such ordinary common sense that we can hardly say he invented it, but he was unique and original in insisting on its rigorous and exclusive application.

The consequences of this attitude appear throughout the Buddha's mature teaching. 'Know not by hearsay, nor by tradition . . . nor by indulgence in speculation . . . nor because you honour [the word of] an ascetic; but know for yourselves' (A I 189). The Buddha's monks were not to speculate about the future or the past, or about such recondite questions as the beginning or end of the world. They were to limit their concern and efforts to one thing, the arising and cessation of suffering within 'this fathom-long carcass'. There are many possible kinds of knowledge, asserted the Buddha, but only those touching this immediate experience were of relevance to his disciples in their search for liberation.

In the Buddha's own search this attitude of circumscribed pragmatism was however not merely a matter of clinging blindly to meditative practices alone. It also led him to reject outright the sort of theories which must have accompanied his yogic teachers' practices. This is not surprising, for, after all, meditative practices must be carried out in the light of some theory of their purpose, of the human constitution and its spiritual environment, and if the techniques fail then doubt must be cast on the theories themselves. We do not of course know just what his teachers' theories were, but we may be fairly certain that they fell within the range of yogic/Upanishadic thought. Moreover, it is clear from those discourses in which the Buddha assails such theories that they shared, from his point of view, certain common characteristics. They were all theories of the Self (Sanskrit *ātman*), though the term used for that indwelling personal principle might have differed from system to system.

At issue was the peculiarly yogic conception of knowledge. For the knowledge of the Self promulgated in such systems was radically different from other sorts of knowledge. From the yogic point of view the knower (the Self) is identical with the known (the Self), and these in turn are identical with the knower's frame of mind.

To get the measure of this let us begin with a contrasting example of ordinary knowledge, that of a skilled goldsmith. (Such examples were frequently used by the Buddha himself, since they already have stamped on them his peculiarly pragmatic turn of mind.) In this case there can be no doubt that the knower, the goldsmith, is inherently different from what he knows. As a craftsman and as a knowing subject he is clearly to be distinguished from his knowledge of the gold, of its properties and uses, and of the skills by which gold may be manipulated. Though we might admit that he would not be much of a goldsmith without the knowledge, we would never in the ordinary course of things be tempted to say that he was identical with his knowledge. The man is one thing, the knowledge another.

Nor would we be tempted to say that a goldsmith's frame of mind was identical with the goldsmith himself. A goldsmith might be angry and upset, or tranquil and alert, and he would still be a goldsmith. Nor, again, would we confuse his frame of mind with his knowledge. Whether angry or tranquil he would still have the knowledge of goldsmithing. In the case of the goldsmith the knower, the known and the frame of mind are clearly separate things even if associated in one goldsmith.

But the introspective yogic knowledge of the Self is quite another matter. For, in the first place, in this yogic knowledge the knower is the same as the known: the Self with a capital 'S', that which is to be known, is the same as the knowing self with a small 's': indeed the Upanishadic texts which proclaim this do not differentiate between the two senses of 'self'. To 'know' oneself in this yogic sense is also to 'attain' or 'become' one's

Self. The power of the Upanishadic vision lies precisely here, in that the witness, the subject of knowledge, reaches a condition in which it witnesses only itself. It is a vision of radical simplification, of the perfect self-identity of the Self. 'There is in it [the Self] no diversity' (B IV 4 19). To realise this Self the yogi has only to turn inward upon himself.

This radical simplification has other consequences as well. Since there is no duality of perceived and perceiver, there are also no perceivable or analysable qualities in the Self (B IV 4 13). If, for example, what is to be realised in meditation is the Self as (meditative) Bliss – one Upanishadic formulation – then the Self is, from the point of view of the meditator, identical with Bliss. The Bliss cannot be separated out, distinguished, from the Self. Or again, if the Self to be realised is the 'Self without qualities' (perhaps in what Buddhists would call a Meditative Plane), then there is no frame of mind 'without qualities' separate from the Self; for in the Self there is 'no diversity'. One can see the plausibility of this from the yogi's point of view, for in accomplished states of meditation he may feel precisely this sense of *becoming* an object of meditation, of total simplification of his experience.

Moreover, such an experience of radical simplification also implies the immutability of the Self: for, since the Self is so perfectly unified, it cannot be thought of as changing, as losing old qualities and taking on new ones. Indeed the 'Self without qualities' could never, by its very definition, be shown to change. And to say immutable is to say eternal. The Buddha's answer to this was that, precisely because such meditative states stop sometime, they cannot be eternal: but for a meditator bolstered by the conviction that what he sought was eternal, the very experience of stability and simplification in meditation would confirm the conviction of eternity. It would confirm as well the conviction that this eternal, immutable, radically simple Self was beyond the world of cause and effect, uncreated, 'unborn' (B IV 4 20). It could not be analysed, broken down into constituent parts (B IV 4 13). It would for him be the all-embracing and undifferentiated 'ground of the universe' (*Brahman*).

The Self, in short, is an eternal, seamless whole, self-identical, beyond phenomenal appearances and unanalysable, yet to be achieved and known through yogic meditation. This yogic vision was a powerful and persuasive one, perhaps precisely because it cut through all the diversity and potential confusion of ordinary experience and offered at a stroke a decisively simple view of the ultimate reality. Any one feature of the vision – the experience of deep meditation, the question of what lies beyond the painful world of appearances, or the nature of Self-knowledge – leads inexorably towards each of its other features. It is no wonder that, despite the Buddha's best efforts, its career continued and expanded in Hindu India.

But, on the other hand, once one bit of it begins to unravel, the rest follows swiftly. We can reconstruct how the Buddha's pragmatic reasoning about meditation led him to reject the Self theories through a discourse in which the Buddha replies to the questions of the ascetic Poṭṭhapāda (D I 185 ff.). If – to pick up the thread at the experience of deep meditation – the meditator is able to witness the Self directly and thereby attain knowledge of it, it could be asked, and was asked by Poṭṭhapāda, whether the frame of mind of deep meditation arises first, and only afterwards the knowledge of the Self appropriate to that frame of mind, or whether the knowledge of the Self comes first, and then the frame of mind, or whether they are simultaneous. That is, could Poṭṭhapāda expect to reach some meditative state and then cast about for the Self, or would the attainment of the state automatically entail the attainment of the Self?

To this the Buddha quite plausibly answered that a particular consciousness or frame of mind arises first, and then the knowledge which accompanies that consciousness. This is the Buddha's meditative pragmatism speaking. For the skilled meditator, having trained to achieve that consciousness, 'knows that it is from such and such conditions that such a consciousness has arisen in me'. The meditator's practical skill is in manipulating the causes and conditions in himself which give rise to progressively more refined states of consciousness. It is upon that achievement, and upon the practical knowledge of introspective psychology that goes with it, that his eventual knowledge of the Self rests.

One can see how even the yogic teachers might have given away this much, for after all there is a good deal of training and skill, and of practical advice to go with it, in any meditative system. But once this is admitted the whole yogic system begins to crumble. For from this radically practical point of view the meditative state, caused and conditioned by the yogi's training, cannot be equivalent to an uncaused, unborn, unanalysable Self: the state itself is quite analysable and clearly caused by something.

In the discourse the Buddha continues to spin out the implications of this pragmatism. Poṭṭhapāda asks another question: 'is the consciousness or frame of mind the same as the Self, or are the Self and the consciousness different?' To this the Buddha posed the counter-question, 'but what is the Self you profess to believe in?' The sense of this question lies in the fact that, though the basic form of Self-theories were the same from the Buddha's point of view, there were evidently many variants in the theory. Different theories might place their version of the Self in rather different spiritual landscapes, or one theory might contain a teaching of several increasingly refined Selves leading up to the ultimate one. So Poṭṭhapāda first offered this: 'I profess a material Self, having a specific form, made of the four elements and nourished by solid food.' The Buddha then replied that 'if there were such a material Self, then the frame of mind and the Self would be different; . . . for even granting such a Self, still some frames of mind would come into being, and others would pass away'. When Poṭṭhapāda then changed tack, and proposed first a Self made not of material, but of mind-stuff, and then one of consciousness alone, the Buddha reiterated his argument; the Self so constituted must be one thing, the frame of mind or state of consciousness quite another. And the reason for this is quite clear: by a yogic definition the Self, whether it is material, immaterial or made of consciousness, must be eternal, unchanging and independent of the causes and conditions of this world. But it is a fact of meditative experience that states of consciousness come and go, for reasons that the meditator himself can understand and, to some limited extent, control. So whatever might be eternal, it is not the states of consciousness, and they must therefore be different from the eternal Self.

The Buddha was aided in this judgment by the use of a word which he took into his vocabulary and made his own. The root meaning of the word (*saṃkhata*) is something like 'prepared' or 'composed'. It covers a rather wider field than 'prepared', however, and in fact it has two meanings which are relevant here: it means 'willed' or 'intended' and it also means 'caused' or 'conditioned'. Meditative states are *saṃkhata*. They are attained by the will or intention of the meditator, and this also means that they are caused and conditioned. They are attributable to certain preceding causes and dependent on certain contemporaneous conditions being fulfilled. As such they are not at all 'unborn', nor are they independent of circumstances.

One might speculate that this is as far as he took his

investigation of meditation and the Self at the time of his encounter with the yoga teachers, but in his mature teaching the Buddha unravels their theory of the Self a great deal further; so far, in fact, that he was to reject it entirely and propose in its place the characteristic Buddhist doctrine of non-self, *anatta*, the absence of an eternal, independent Self, whether in ordinary consciousness, in meditative states or anywhere else. This teaching was well integrated with his other thought on both ethics and psychology. In his mature view this eternal Self could not be witnessed at all, and those who believe in it are likened to a man who says that he is in love with the most beautiful woman in the land, but is unable to specify her name, her family or her appearance (D I 193).

This eternal Self is, in other words, a product of speculation, of falsely understood meditative experience, or of hearsay. The Buddha was willing to admit the existence of a self – and here the lower-case 's' is very appropriate – but that self was merely 'an agreed term, a common form of words, a worldly usage, a practical designation' (D I 202). One could reasonably say 'discipline yourself' or 'know yourself', but in so saying one would not be assuming the existence of an eternal entity. The Buddha drew an analogy with milk. Milk can become curds, then butter, and then ghee, but there would be no point in speaking of an abiding entity (milkness?) which would persist through these changes: milk is just milk, butter just butter. The British scholar T. W. Rhys Davids put it in these terms:

when the change (in the composition of the personality) has reached a certain point, it is convenient to change the designation, the name, by which the personality is known – just as in the products of the cow. But the abstract term is only a convenient *form of expression*. There never was any personality, *as a separate entity*, all the time.

So when we say, 'I feel as if I am a different person today', we are in fact alluding to an important truth about human nature.

This is a difficult doctrine, and a courageous one, in that it led into waters uncharted by the meditators of the Buddha's time. One difficulty is that of purely intellectual understanding. When the Buddha went on to develop a new method of meditation it was aimed at analysing in detail the self (small 's') of the meditator. By this method one could see how this self was in fact 'composed', made up from previous causes and subsisting on contemporaneous conditions. The doctrine in detail is one of formidable complexity, but its basic principle is simple. Just as milk progressively changes, so the self which we experience changes continually for specifiable reasons.

The real difficulty is not, however, one of intellectual understanding, but of emotional plausibility. Anyone might ask with alarm: how can I, with my well-developed sense of myself, be expected to accept that I have no self? The intellectual answer is that one has a self, but no eternal Self. But it is the emotional answer which is important. Since anyone attempting to attain or witness an eternal unchanging Self was, in the Buddha's view, bound to failure, the doctrine of the Self was an invitation to further suffering: 'such [a doctrine of the eternal Self] is merely a sensation, a writhing in discomfort, of those venerable ascetics and Brahmans who neither know nor see, and who have fallen victim to desire [for such a Self]' (D I 40–1). So to give up such a doctrine was to give up a potent source of frustration. The emotional tone of the teaching of non-self was that of a calm and relieved detachment. It was a liberation which transcended the frustrated strivings of those who revolve around a Self 'like a dog tied to a post' (M II 232–3).

*

But let us return for the moment to that point at which the

Buddha realised that these yogic systems of meditation in their very nature led to mutable states of consciousness quite different from their avowed object, the eternal Self. From such a conclusion two further consequences might follow. One is that there is indeed no eternal Self, and that is the path the Buddha eventually took. The other is that the Self exists, but is not to be obtained by yogic methods. Another discipline, however, might lead to its achievement, and there was such a discipline at hand: the method of self-mortification and extreme asceticism which we know best through Jainism. On such a view the eternal principle in the individual, called the *jīva*, the 'life' or 'soul', is held in the world of suffering by the effects of transgressions committed in earlier lives, and these effects adhere to the soul like dirt. By avoiding further transgressions one obviates further bondage in the world of suffering, and by self-mortification and voluntary penances one burns away the effects of former transgressions from the soul, so that it rises to bliss and eternal freedom from pain. Here there is no necessity for meditation, nor for the application of introspective knowledge, though the theory probably did hold, as Jainism does, that knowledge, indeed omniscience, would miraculously result from the successful prosecution of such asceticism.

So after leaving Uddaka Rāmaputta, the yogic teacher, the Buddha turned to self-mortification, and the canonical discourses leave no doubt about the sincerity of his efforts in this direction. He stopped breathing completely, so that 'violent winds racked my head . . . and violent winds carved up my belly, as a skilled butcher . . . carves up an ox's belly with a sharp knife' (M I 244). Passing deities thought he was dead. Then he gave up eating more than a handful of food daily, so that 'my spine stood out like a corded rope, my ribs projected like the jutting rafters of an old roofless cowshed, and the light of my eyes sunk down in their sockets looked like the gleam of water sunk in a deep well' (M I 245). Passersby thought him a black man, so much had his austerities affected his clear complexion. By the extremity of these exertions the Buddha came to the conclusion that 'in the past, present, or future, whatever ascetic or Brahman might experience such painful, racking, and piercing feelings, he will not exceed this' (M I 246).

But he also came to the conclusion that 'by these gruelling exertions I have by no means gone beyond the common human condition to an eminence of knowledge and vision appropriate to those who are truly (spiritually) noble'. Or, in other words, all he had to show for it was a prominent rib cage. 'There must be another path to wisdom.'

*

In the traditional narrative this conclusion brought the Buddha to the threshold of awakening. But it also brings us to substantial difficulties in the interpretation of the sources. For, on the one hand, the Buddha is represented in the narrative as having reached, in a relatively short time, the saving knowledge, the certainty that 'birth is exhausted, the ascetic's life has been consummated, what was to be done has been done' (M I 249). Indeed the awakening is meant to have taken place within one night. However, it is already clear that the Buddha's progress towards awakening was long and complex, a process in which he gradually transformed himself by various disciplines and worked out an acceptable view of himself and the world. This was recognised in later discourses: 'just as the ocean slopes gradually, falls away gradually, shelves gradually, with no sudden drop, so in this teaching the training, the practice, the path are gradual, with no sudden penetration of knowledge' (A IV 200–1).

How are we to resolve this contradiction? In the first place, we must accept that the purely biographical narratives are compressed accounts: they are stories, and they are stories which march at a smart pace. Their material was meant not only to be historical, but to be an inspiration to later disciples, so they were fitted into a relatively manageable span. They had dramatic tension. Hence, even if we accept that the awakening, as a moment of certainty in the Buddha's mind that he was indeed on the right path, did take place on a single night, that certainty was long in the making and longer in the elaboration of its implications.

In the traditional account the Buddha, realising the pointlessness of extreme asceticism, accepted a reasonable meal and sat down to find that other path. In effect, that is, he accepted a still relatively disciplined asceticism, but one which avoided extremes of sensual indulgence or of self-mortification. He was soon to designate this more measured asceticism as the 'Middle Path'.

He also recollected a time when, as a child, he had sat under a rose-apple tree while his father had worked in the fields. He had on that occasion entered the first Absorption, 'accompanied with casual and applied thought, and with bodily happiness and the mental pleasure born of seclusion'. And he recognised that 'this might well be the way to awakening' (M I 246).

This account alludes only indirectly to the Buddha's original meditative accomplishments before the awakening. These accomplishments were composed, on the one hand, of his already established habit of meditative pragmatism, of his concentration upon what he could witness by, and within, himself; and on the other, of his now hardened inclination to analysis and criticism. For despite his rejection of the yogis' doctrine, he continued to cultivate the awareness of mental and physical states, an awareness which had arisen out of the yogis' psychic technology. If it was impossible to find an enduring entity, a Self with a capital 'S', through and behind these mutable experiences, it was possible at least to have an insight into the nature of these evanescent psychophysical processes themselves. Here were matters which could be directly witnessed and directly understood, and it was upon these processes that the Buddha turned the full weight of his concentration and driving curiosity. For if he could not find a Self, he could at least find release.

What these efforts gave rise to was a distinguishable meditative skill, quite different from that practised by other yogis. For this concern with immediate experience required not only a power of concentration, but also a kind of mindfulness and self-possession through which the Buddha could in fact see what was going on in his mind and body. Indeed it was just these qualities, mindfulness and self-possession (*sati-sampajañña*), which were to be taught throughout the Buddha's mature discourses. They demanded the ability to witness here and now with full lucidity the inner and outer states of oneself (and, by extension, the analogous experiences of others). The single most important text for the training of his own disciples was to be the Great Discourse on the Foundations of Mindfulness (D II 290 ff.), and these foundations are the dispassionate, immediate and clear perceptions of the meditator's own body, feelings, state of mind and mental contents. Such alert perceptions presupposed to an extent the one-pointedness and equanimity of the Absorptions, but they required at the same time a bright awareness of the smallest perception. This emphasis on, and elaboration of, wakeful and energetic introspection constituted the Buddha's unique contribution to meditative technology. From the conclusions based on this introspection the awakening was to flow.

How can one treat objectively, and analyse, one's own

immediate feelings and attitudes? Would not the effort to per-
ceive passions dispassionately, for example, destroy the object
of study itself? The answer to these questions lies in the course
of training to which the Buddha had already subjected
himself, albeit unsystematically, in his search. In the pursuit
of both meditative accomplishments and asceticism the
Buddha had repeatedly disciplined himself to ignore those
sensations and impulses which ordinarily issue in action or
reaction, and which would thereby have deflected him from
his purpose. He had ignored the calls of hunger and thirst
which accompanied his fast, as he ignored those pains of the
body and distractions of the mind which accompany long and
arduous meditation. The effect of such long discipline – as
meditators today attest – is not only to achieve a reproduce-
able tranquillity, but also to break long-standing, automatic
and unconscious habits. One would ordinarily break a fast to
eat, but the ascetic does not. One would ordinarily shift from a
physical position which grows increasingly uncomfortable,
but the meditator does not. To get the measure of this
meditation, try this experiment: sit in the most comfortable
possible position in a comfortable chair, and try to hold that
position without moving for an hour. The Buddhist predic-
tion is that within minutes you will wish to scratch the nose,
twitch the finger, shift the leg. What if one could watch these
urges arise and pass away with no movement at all?

But this is not to say that impulses to respond to such calls
disappear, for they do not, or at least not permanently. In the
meditator such impulses simply do not issue in a reaction. He
is tranquil, his mind is malleable (*kammañña*). He can temporarily ignore such impulses completely if he chooses, as
in an Absorption, but his long-term relationship to such
impulses is also changed, for he can now respond to such
impulses in a reasoned rather than an automatic way.

51

Moreover, just because such sensations and impulses do not disappear, he can choose to exercise mindfulness, securely founded in his now habitual equanimity, to observe and analyse them. Whereas the ordinary unskilled person can with clarity contemplate painful or pleasurable sensations, and the accompanying impulses and emotions, only in the tranquillity of memory, safely removed from their effects by time, the meditator learns to do so immediately, as they actually occur. It must be the case that, because of his long training, the meditating ascetic perceives his pains, pleasures and urges as being less poignant and pressing, but this does not change their fundamental nature. And in any case the meditator may still use memory, and the observation of other people, to confirm that what he observes of his relatively controlled emotions must also be true of less controlled emotions.

This new form of meditation was to be called insight (*vipassanā*) meditation. It was the Buddha's experimental method, his way of gathering information, and upon this information about his presently occurring states of body and mind his analysis of the human condition was to be erected.

4 The awakening

In Buddhist countries the awakening is thought to have occurred on a single night of the full moon of the lunar month Vesakha, April – May, as the Buddha sat beneath a huge Bodhi tree (*ficus religiosus*). With the awakening (*sambodhi*) the Buddha attained, first, a knowledge of the nature of the human condition that would lead to salvation and, second, the certainty that he himself had attained liberation from the sorrows of that condition. The early scriptures attribute many doctrines, and certainly the most important ones, to the night of the awakening itself, so that the awakening is made to bear the weight of the whole of the Buddha's mature teaching. Even if this is not literally true, the knowledge and certainty of that night must lie at the base of the mature teaching.

The awakening grew out of a creative tension between two governing convictions. One was that the answer was to be sought in painstaking attention to the minutiae of experience as witnessed in insight meditation (though the articulated method of that meditation may not yet have been fully formed). But if this consideration alone had informed the Buddha, he might have become only a minor contributor to yogic thought. The other conviction, however, was that of the truth of transmigration, and the Buddha's conception of this gave his teaching a scope and a purchasing power in human life which transcended the narrow yogic concerns. The Buddha's originality stemmed from his close analysis of individual experience, but his importance stemmed from his acceptance of this common Indian belief in rebirth.

In the Buddha's case this belief came down to a deep moral

53

seriousness. In other teachings the doctrine of transmigration went with an elaborate view of the spiritual cosmos within which transmigration occurs. One moves up and down, becoming now an animal, now a god, now the denizen of some hell, and again a Warrior or Brahman, a slave or a king (Buddhism itself was later to be prolific in the production of such views). But for the Buddha the specific details of transmigration were never so important as the principle underlying it: human action has moral consequences, consequences which are inescapable, returning upon one whether in this life or another. There *is* a fundamental moral order. One cannot steal, lie, commit adultery or 'go along the banks of the Ganges striking, slaying, mutilating and commanding others to mutilate, oppressing and commanding others to oppress' (D I 52), without reaping the consequences. There *is* an impersonal moral causation to which all are subjected. Misdeeds lead to misery in this life or in later lives. The Buddha's teaching was devoted to the apparently selfish purpose of self-liberation, being directed to sentient beings in so far as they are capable of misery and final liberation from misery. But the teaching also touched sentient beings as moral agents, as agents capable of affecting the welfare not only of themselves but of others as well. Some of his teachings seem to treat only personal liberation, others morality, but for the Buddha the two matters were always intimately and necessarily connected.

The teaching most closely connected with the awakening chiefly concerns personal misery and personal liberation. This is the doctrine of the Four Noble Truths (*cattāri ariyasaccāni*), which cover under their spacious umbrella the central tenets of Buddhism. These are phrased after the pattern of a medical diagnosis: this is the disease, these are the causes of the disease, this is the judgment of whether it is curable, this is the method of treatment. The disease is 'suffering' (*dukkha*) – a condition which covers all that is meant in English by 'suffering' but more as well, and this wider sphere of meaning must be borne in mind. The first Noble Truth is that there does indeed exist the disease, suffering, and this is the Truth of Suffering. The second Noble Truth is that there are discernible causes of suffering: this is the Noble Truth of the Arising of Suffering, which contains an account of those causes. The third Noble Truth is that there is in fact a cure for suffering, and this is the Truth of the Cessation of Suffering. The fourth Noble Truth is that of the cure for suffering, the Truth of the Path Leading to the Cessation of Suffering.

Let us take the first Truth, that of the existence of suffering, in a form in which the Buddha is traditionally thought to have explained it shortly after the awakening. That description begins thus: 'What is the Noble Truth of Suffering? Birth is suffering, ageing is suffering, sorrow and lamentation, pain, grief, and despair are suffering' (S V 421). Here there is no problem in translating *dukkha* as 'suffering'. This is suffering viewed as we might commonly view it, on a large time-scale, a concomitant of any human life as a whole: in so far as we are born, we are bound to suffer in being born, in sickness, in growing old, in the loss of loved ones and in death. This long-term view considers that the continuous process of birth and death could not be anything but a magnification in one life after another of the sorrow which falls to any one human life. All our experience, even that of common happiness, is bracketed by pain and sorrow. Since in the long run we are all dead, the problem of suffering is a pressing one, demanding a solution.

At this level the Truth of Suffering resembles other views, common among renouncers, that worldly life is a morass of pain. But what saves it from conventional pessimism is its connection with a more carefully worked-out view of human fate. This view is progressively revealed as the description of the Truth of Suffering continues: 'association with what is disliked is suffering, dissociation from what is desired is suffering, not to get what one wants is suffering'. This is suffering on a more intimate time-scale, as it might appear within a year, a day or even an hour, and is closer to the Buddha's characteristic concern with what is immediately observable. It is also a more general description of suffering, not only as it accompanies the crises of life, but as it appears in everyday situations, situations which might not occasion lamentation but rather an acute consciousness of failure, or of frustration, or of unfulfilled yearning: the missed opportunity, the baffled effort, the irksome routine, the petty irritation of life with others. Here *dukkha* might be translated not as 'suffering', but as something less grand but more pervasive: discomfort, dissatisfaction or discontent. This is illustrated in the canon by tales of, for example, the insecurity of office-seekers, the anxieties of husbandmen, the irritations and frustrations of household life. This teaching brings suffering within the ambit of daily experience, for it points to the inescapably changing nature of life, which engulfs all the things we believe to be secure and stable.

But such a viewpoint was also shared with others at the Buddha's time, so for a doctrine which is quite uniquely Buddhist, we shall have to turn to the end of this description of the first Truth: 'in sum, all the aspects of experience in the mind and body . . . are suffering'. This is the definition of suffering which leads to the heart of what is original in the Buddha's teaching, and to that part of his view of suffering which is thoroughly argued in the canonical sources as a dispassionate description of the human plight. Here suffering is seen as being woven most finely into the texture of human experience; here experience is considered on the smallest time-scale, from second to second, under a microscope, under the clinical eye of the introspecting meditator. Under this microscope *dukkha* falls within another range of meanings, such as imperfection, impermanence, evanescence, inadequacy, insubstantiality, incompleteness, uncontrollability. The great crises which occasion lamentation, and the small desperations which occasion discontent, are but especially visible examples of the fundamental imperfection-cum-impermanence – suffering – which is inherent in all experience. In so far as it is dynamic, changing, uncontrollable and not finally satisfactory, experience is itself precisely suffering.

To see how this works let us take the case of feeling (*vedanā*) as a paradigm. Feeling is one of the objects of immediate introspection recommended in insight meditation, and it is also one of the 'aspects of experience in the mind and body'. Feeling may be physical or mental, and it may be adjudged pleasant, unpleasant or neither pleasant nor unpleasant, i.e. neutral. So, as he contemplates his presently occurring experience, the insight meditator is to discern, as each actually arises, that this feeling is pleasant, or that feeling unpleasant, or another feeling quite neutral. For example, the pains in one's knees as one tries to sit cross-legged in meditation are unpleasant; the exhilaration of actually managing to sit for a long period and gain some concentration is pleasant; and many feelings in between, such as that of the process of calm breathing, are neutral. Or again, the blowing of a car horn just outside the room in which one is meditating might occasion unpleasant feelings, the song of a nightingale might occasion pleasant ones, or the sound of rain might occasion neither. Though some of the feelings which thus arise and clamour for attention may last for a while – such as the pains in the knees – or may come back again and again, it does not require deep meditative insight to see why the Buddha came to regard feelings as impermanent. They are soon chased away by other feelings, and even in the great meditative attainments cannot be made to abide. The question which underlay the Buddha's quest was, 'in what may I place lasting reliance?' On this diagnosis, certainly not in feeling, for even pleasant feelings are 'suffering by virtue of change'; that is, though pleasant at the moment, they bear within them the seed of insecurity, of their own imminent destruction. The introspectively discovered Truth of Suffering is one of ceaseless movement, of a dynamic process which is suffering by virtue of being uncontrollable, ever-changing, and therefore inadequate and unsatisfying.

Furthermore this inadequacy rules throughout the experience of both the mind and body of the individual. The Buddha proposed several different analytic descriptions of the mind and body, each fitted to a different context; but generally these descriptions are of a process, not a stable entity. The individual is seen by the Buddha more as, say, a burning fire or a swiftly moving stream than as a solid vessel for holding experience or an unmoving slate upon which perceptions are written. Our own language tends to obscure this, for we tend to think of a relatively stable body and mind which receive a dynamic and changing experience, and we therefore tend to think that mind and body can be described apart from experience. But the Buddha's language was one in which both experience and the mind-body complex were described together, as part of a single process. Here, for example, is such a description:

In dependence upon the eye and upon visible objects visual consciousness arises. The union of these three [i.e. the eye, objects, and visual consciousness] constitutes contact. Dependent upon this contact feeling is constituted. One perceives what is thus felt; what one perceives one considers; and what one considers one develops all sorts of notions about. (M I 111–12)

In this view, objects of experience, the organs of experience such as the eye, and the consequent consciousness of experience, 'the mind', are indissolubly linked. None of the three is conceivable without the other: they lean upon each other as one sheaf of reeds leans upon another, to use a canonical simile.

Furthermore, those features of experience which might be said to lie within the 'mind' itself, such as perception, feeling and consciousness, are themselves 'conjoined, not disjoined, and it is impossible to separate them in order to specify their individual characteristics' (M I 293). So right from the objects of perception, through the physical organs of perception, to feeling, consciousness, thought and volition, there is one dynamic, interdependent, ever-changing complex, which might be called an 'individual' or a 'self', but which has nothing lasting in it.

Indeed the very term which I have translated as 'all aspects of experience in the mind and body' is one of the analytic descriptions of this process, a description in which the impersonal, dynamic and interdependent nature of the process is already implicit. This term is the 'five aggregates' (*pañcakkhanda*). The first 'aggregate' is materiality, which includes physical objects, the body, and sense organs. The other four 'aggregates' are feeling, perceptions, impulses and consciousness. Within these 'aggregates', this process, are included all that pertains to an individual and his experience. Feeling is but one face of this process, a face available to insight meditation. The mutability and inadequacy of feeling are characteristic of the whole process: 'all aspects of experience in the mind and body are suffering'. Or, as the Buddha said elsewhere, 'as the aggregates arise, decay, and die,

O monk, so from moment to moment you are born, decay, and die' (P I 78).

This seems a gloomy doctrine, and a common instinct is to question it. Surely there must be some happiness in the world? However, the Buddha's teaching does not deny that there are satisfactions in experience: the exercise of insight assumes that the meditator sees such happiness clearly. Pain is to be seen as pain, pleasure as pleasure. What is denied is that such happiness will be secure and lasting.

But this does not fully answer the doubt, for the real grounds of it lie elsewhere, in a radical difference between the experience of the questioner and that of the Buddha. The doctrine of suffering presupposes a vulnerability to disease, death, natural calamity and human oppression that characterised the Buddha's world, as it does much of the world today. It is in these terms that the doctrine is illustrated in the canon. But for many in the societies of the West this vulnerability is suppressed or rendered inconspicuous – by prosperity, by medical advances and by those peculiar institutions surrounding death which render it invisible. Without that sense of vulnerability there might be little reason to connect suffering as unsatisfactoriness on the small scale, with death, disease and lasting failure on the grand scale: one could just put up with the discomforts (as indeed Buddhist monks learn to do). However, for those whose experience includes vulnerability – a vulnerability that might be psychological or social as well as material – the connection can have a compelling cogency.

*

Though the announcement of the Four Noble Truths is in fact brief and bare, there is a good deal of dramatic tension in it. For if suffering is such a pervasive and unending process, what could be its cause? How could one break into the cycle to see what makes it revolve? And from this point of view the discovery of the second Noble Truth (that there are discernible causes of suffering), the Truth of the Arising of Suffering, is the centre-piece of the awakening. Some Buddhists celebrate this as a dramatic moment in which the Buddha saw the 'house-builder', the cause of this flawed and unsatisfactory existence. He is said on that occasion to have uttered this verse:

> Seeking but not finding the house-builder
> I travelled through life after life.
> How painful is repeated birth!
> House-builder, you have now been seen.
> You will not build the house again.
>
> (*Dhammapada* 153–4)

We can already see the directions in which the Buddha would look for this cause. One direction is given by the Buddha's pragmatic turn of mind. He tended to think of causes not in a purely abstract way, but rather by using analogies from practical activity. The meditator, for example, is likened to a goldsmith, or to a fletcher straightening the mind like an arrow. In one passage (M I 240–3), concerning the Buddha's search before the awakening, he speaks of his efforts on the analogy of a man trying to start a fire: just as a man could not start a fire by rubbing a dry stick upon a wet one lying in water, or by rubbing it upon a wet stick lying on dry land, but only by rubbing a dry stick on another dry stick on dry land, so a meditator must be *bodily* withdrawn from sensual pleasures (a stick out of water), and also *mentally* withdrawn from such pleasures (a *dry* stick out of water). This way of thinking has a good deal of subtlety in it, for it recognises that there are subsidiary, enabling causes and conditions, such as the dryness of the stick and so forth. But it places the chief cause with the agent, the meditator, the man making the fire. The chief cause is conceived as being *agent-like*, like a person bringing about a result. This is certainly the sense of describing the cause of suffering metaphorically as the 'house-builder'. The pieces of that 'house' had to be lying to hand, but there also had to be a 'builder', a *purposive* and *active* principle. Hence, in seeking the cause of suffering, the Buddha was seeking something active and purposive, which was to that extent like an agent, a person.

Moreover, this principle had to be agent-like in other ways as well. First, just as the meditator can, to an extent, control himself in order to perfect his meditative skill, so this principle had to respond to corrective action. Like a person or agent, it had to be corrigible: it had to be possible to deal with the 'house-builder' as one deals with oneself, for otherwise there would be no possibility of liberation. Second, just because the activities of this principle had moral consequences, upon others and upon oneself in the process of rebirth, it had to be like a *moral agent*, a person whose acts are good or evil. These considerations may seem so abstract as to be inconsistent with the Buddha's pragmatism, but they point to the practical obstacle he had to overcome. The simplest explanation of all this might be just that the purposive, active principle is an agent, a Self or 'person' or soul. But the Buddha had good reason for rejecting this idea. Indeed in his insight meditation he had found only an *impersonal* process, that of suffering. He had to break through to find a principle which was in many ways like an agent or person, but which was finally impersonal, not an agent or person at all.

This is what he discovered:

And this, O monks, is the Truth of the Arising of Suffering. It is just thirst or craving [*taṇhā*] which gives rise to repeated existence, which is bound up with impassioned appetite, and which seeks fresh pleasure now here and now there, namely, thirst for sensual pleasures, thirst for existence, thirst for non-existence. (S V 421)

So thirst or craving is that which drives the whole mass of suffering experience forward. The word *taṇhā* bears the literal sense of 'thirst', and it is this meaning that lends the term its vividness. Its technical sense, however, is 'craving' or 'desire'. In this sense it is insatiable craving, 'which seeks fresh pleasure now here and now there', not only in this life but in the lives beyond, and because of this it 'gives rise to repeated existence'. Moreover, in so far as craving is 'bound up with impassioned appetite', the metaphor of fire was never far from the Buddha's mind, and indeed in a discourse traditionally placed very early in his career, the Fire Sermon (S IV 19), each facet of experience is described as 'aflame with desire'.

This way of thinking is in many ways poetical rather than soberly technical, and a good deal of the Buddha's effort around and after the awakening must have been devoted to drawing out the implications of this pregnant idea. Certainly craving could be shown to be purposive: to crave is to crave something, to be thirsty is to be thirsty *for* something. 'Where does this craving come into being and settle itself? Wherever there is what seems lovable and gratifying, there it comes into being and settles' (D II 308). In most descriptions of craving there is a tendency to emphasise this positive desire, 'desire for sensual pleasure'. This was the puritanism of the renouncers speaking. Indeed, the idea of desire was common among the renouncers: it was the great obstacle to achieving the Self or purifying the soul. But in elevating it to an autonomous principle the Buddha expanded its definition. For him craving also included aversion, and that is probably the sense of 'thirst for non-existence'. One craves not only what is attractive but also relief or escape from what is unpleasant or undesirable. And we crave a great deal. We crave all sensual pleasures – sexual, gustatory, olfactory, tactile or whatever. We yearn keenly to escape pain. We crave wealth, power, position. We even lust sensually after our own bodies, or in rebirth a new body. There is even a 'thirst for views', the urge to be right, to be in the know, to have an answer for every question.

Craving may be spoken of comprehensively as 'thirst for existence'. This is, to be sure, the 'thirst which gives rise to repeated existence', but perhaps a better way to think of it is as *the desire for becoming other than what present experience gives*. Under many guises it is a ceaseless striving for some new state, some new being, some new experience, at the same time as being a striving for satiety and permanence, and it is a striving always frustrated. 'The world [in the sense of all common individuals in the world], whose nature is to become other, is committed to becoming, has exposed itself to becoming; it relishes only becoming, yet what it relishes brings fear, and what it fears is pain' (U III 10, Ñānamoli's reading). Rebirth may be rebirth from moment to moment of experience, or it may be rebirth in another life, but in either case it is the consequence of this lust *to be something else*.

This is the purposive activity of craving on a large scale, as it embraces all sentient life. But this grand vision is to be justified, as ever in the Buddha's teaching, by reference to the fine grain of experience. In this perspective craving was in fact already written into the five 'aggregates', that comprehensive description of mental and physical experience, as impulses (*saṃkhārā*). Let us return to the example of the pains in the knees one feels when trying to sit for long periods in insight meditation. Just because one feels these as unpleasant, one also feels an urge to change position, an impulse to seek comfort and relief by moving. This impulse is, in effect, just the active, purposive aspect of the unpleasant feeling: it arises with the unpleasant feeling, is indeed inseparable from it. In ordinary circumstances one would simply shift position automatically, without reflecting or perhaps even without being conscious of it. The same might be said for pleasant feelings: while meditating one might feel sleepy and dreamy, and one is moved automatically to follow and indulge such feelings. Or one feels hungry and thinks of having a little snack before continuing. Without the attempt at meditation many such impulses would hardly be noticed, so instantly do they follow one another. In this microscopic view, experience is revealed as having a foundation of ceaseless activity, of short-lived purposive impulses. The Buddha indeed thought of this activity as *making* experience. 'What is called "mentality" and "mind" and "consciousness" arises and ceases, in one way and another, through day and night; just as a monkey ranging through a forest seizes a branch and, letting go, seizes another' (S II 95).

This perception through insight meditation of an animating principle of existence ruled the Buddha's thought. It was the evidence which guided his understanding of the human condition. Because impulse is habitual and automatic, fundamentally unreflective and not a function of decision, there was no reason to think of it as the work of some person or Self, as other renouncers thought. It was just a propensity, an active disposition at the base of life which had the special and disastrous ability to reproduce itself endlessly. As a propensity he called it 'clinging' (*upādāna*). This propensity was in fact already written into the Noble Truth of Suffering, for the full form of that reads: 'all aspects of experience in the mind and body, *in which clinging inheres*, are suffering' (S V 421). The different terms – clinging, craving, impulse, thirst – each shed a different light on the activity behind and within sentient life. They all point to one thing, the impersonal active principle, the discovery of which answered the Buddha's question, 'how did I come to be in this sorry plight?'

The Buddha did not consider, however, that craving acts alone – his idea of causes by no means required a single or a simple solution to the problem. While craving might be the chief motive cause in the painful process of rebirth, there was room for subsidiary, enabling causes, conditions without which it could not take hold. And among these there was one which had an especially important place: ignorance or delusion. The idea was current among the wanderers and yogis: they enjoyed a special knowledge of which others were ignorant. In the Buddha's usage, however, his knowledge was not so much an esoteric truth like the knowledge of the Self, but rather a penetrating understanding of *things as they are*. By comparison people are ordinarily not so much uninformed – as one might be uninformed of tax laws or of the Self – but positively deluded. They hold that the world contains lasting and secure satisfactions, whereas in fact it is riddled with suffering. They are mistaken, so craving has its way with them. The relationship between craving, ignorance and suffering is rather like the relationship between heat, oxygen and fire. Heat is the motive force, but without oxygen fire could not arise. 'Thirst for existence, O monks, has a specific condition; it is nourished by something, it does not go without support. And what is that nourishment? It is ignorance' (A V 116).

*

So far these teachings are amoral. They are the utterances of a detached specialist, a renouncer, addressing himself to others with the same concern for personal salvation. But the Buddha was also convinced that sentient beings are subjected to a law of moral causation, and he was deeply concerned with the evaluation of behaviour and its effects on others. So these amoral teachings are indissolubly linked in his thought with others that point to a radically moral significance in the human condition.

Let us begin with impulses. As I have so far described them impulses hardly have a moral significance, but they may be regarded from another point of view. They may be considered as intentions or choices, both of which are included in the key term *cetanā*. Sometimes 'choice' is the best translation, in so far as it is a mental movement which precedes action or speech. But intentions are also included, for the Buddha thought that unexpressed intentions could themselves have an effect, if not outwardly then inwardly in the mind. The Buddha held that in human affairs it is the mental choice or intention which is of ultimate significance: 'the world is led by mind' (S I 39). Hence, for example, in the legal system developed for the Buddhist order, only intentional actions are regarded as transgressions, and unintentional acts – such as those committed while asleep, or mad, or under duress – are not culpable.

This has great implications. It means that intentions are not negligible, that they have consequences. They do work, are in themselves actions. This is the sense of the term 'karma', whose primary meaning is just 'work' or 'deed', but in this Buddhist sense 'mental action'. (Karma does not refer to the *results* of action, as we now assume in ordinary usage in the West.) 'It is choice or intention that I call karma – mental work –, for having chosen a man acts by body, speech and mind' (A III 415). Intentions make one's world; it is they that do the work whose consequences we must reap in suffering. They form the subsequent history of our psychic life as surely as wars or treaties, plagues or prosperity form the subsequent history of a nation.

To speak of impulses and urges is not necessarily to speak in moral terms, but choices and actions are the very stuff of moral discourse. One may make good or bad choices, one's actions may be good or evil. And in fact from the Buddha's point of view *unconscious* impulses are really to be equated with *conscious* choices, the only difference being that impulses occur in ignorance of their nature as choices: they are choices made under the delusion that there is no better choice, no better way of acting. In this light the relatively neutral term thirst (craving) may itself be considered as greed, something morally reprehensible, and frequently the Buddha spoke in just this way. Greed may be supported by sheer delusion about the nature of the world, but it is also immoral, a propensity to be condemned and, in oneself, to be improved upon. Moreover greed is always coupled in the discourses with hatred or aversion. Hence from a radically moral standpoint it is by choosing badly, by being greedy and hateful, that we bring upon ourselves the suffering we meet in birth after birth. The ill that we cause ourselves and the ill that we cause others are of a piece, stemming from the same roots. The Noble Truth of the Arising of Suffering could be rephrased thus: 'inflamed by greed, incensed by hate, confused by delusion, overcome by them, obsessed in mind, a man chooses for his own affliction, for others' affliction, for the affliction of both, and experiences pain and grief' (A III 55).

Or in other words the propensities of greed, hatred and delusion which cause us to injure others through evil deeds are exactly the same propensities which cause us to suffer ourselves by being reborn in life after life. The moral cause in transmigration is equivalent to the cause of suffering. But this raises a fundamental question: how exactly does this cause work? For a doctrine of a Self or soul it is easy enough. The Self acts, causes consequences to itself, and is reborn again according to its deserts. The basic structure is in its own terms plausible, so the details are not so important. But what if there is no Self?

The answer (as it appears at D II no. 15) works backwards from the appearance of a new body and mind, a new psychophysical entity. How did this appear? It appeared through the descent of consciousness into a mother's womb. On the face of it this is primitive, going back to earlier Indian ideas of an homunculus descending into the womb; and it is speculative, going beyond the Buddha's brief of attending only to what he could witness himself. But later Buddhist commentators are clear that this descent is metaphorical, as we might say 'darkness descended on him' if someone fell unconscious. Moreover this enlivening consciousness is not an independent entity, a disguised Self, but is composed of causes and conditions.

So what in turn were these preceding conditions? One was the act of physical generation, but more important was a previous impulse. Here impulse is to be understood as intention or mental action, bearing a moral quality and informing by that quality the nature of the new psychophysical entity. If the impulse was good the new body and mind will be well endowed and fortunately placed, if not it will be poorly endowed and unfortunate.

And now comes the key question: what is this mysterious impulse? It is in fact nothing other than the final impulse, the dying thought, of the previous mind and body. It is nothing like a Self, but is merely a last energy which leaps the gap from life to life rather like − as a later Buddhist source puts it − a flame leaping from one candle wick to another. Nor is it free of preceding conditions, for it is the product of the dispositions formed by habitual mental actions conducted under the veil of ignorance and desire within the previous life. And thus one can trace the process back − to beginningless time, in fact.

In this account there is no underlying entity, but there is a stream of events which has its own history. This history is borne forward, not by a Self or soul, but by the complex inter-action of the causes, conditions and effects summarised under craving and suffering. To understand this interaction is to understand the nature and origins of the human condition. Many canonical accounts treat this as the substance of the awakening itself: the Buddha called it dependent co-origination (*paṭicca samuppāda*). It was dependent in that the causes and conditions necessarily interact with each other, as do fuel, heat, oxygen and so forth in the production of fire. No one of them is finally independent, as a Self or soul might be. So dependent co-origination served two functions: it refuted the idea of an independent permanent soul, and it described the origin of suffering. The doctrine attached to dependent co-origination includes everything I have discussed under the first two Noble Truths, though it is phrased somewhat differently. It usually (but not always) comprises twelve factors. These range from those describing the psychophysical entity, such as sense organs and feeling, to the descriptions of the sources of suffering, namely ignorance, craving, clinging and impulses. And of course it includes suffering as well. Though we might speculate that, as a doctrine, dependent co-origination appeared after the Four Noble Truths, it was in fact already inherent in them, in the Buddha's understanding of craving and suffering, and of the interactions through which craving causes suffering.

*

The third Noble Truth, the Truth of the Cessation of Suffering, certifies that the disease of suffering is actually curable. Though there is no permanent moral person, the impersonal process is corrigible. One can achieve liberation.

Within the Four Noble Truths this is a relatively colourless doctrine, fulfilling the form of the medical diagnosis. But it did speak to an important body of opinion held at the Buddha's time. This was represented especially by the Ājīvikas, who held that the process of rebirth is an automatic, mechanical one: every being must, whatever he does, be reborn in every possible condition, and every being is destined ultimately to attain salvation, so special effort is pointless. An Ājīvika might well have asked the Buddha whether his own doctrine of dependent co-origination did not in effect lead to just such a conclusion. Do not these causes and conditions, however complex, lead in the end to a mechanically pre-destined result, rather like an intricate clockwork wound up and set ticking? To this the Buddha's answer was that, though one's endowments and capacities are formed by circumstances in previous lives, one still has the ability, within the confines of this present life, to alter voluntarily one's behaviour. One can dispel ignorance by seeing the world as it is, as it is described in the Four Noble Truths. And one can control craving by the measured renouncer's discipline promulgated by the Buddha.

The fourth Noble Truth is the Truth of the Path Leading to the Cessation of Suffering. This contains the prescription, the medicine. This is usually given as the Noble Eightfold Path, but already in canonical sources this list is conveniently broken down into three constituents: moral self-discipline or morality, meditation, and wisdom (*sīla, samādhi, paññā*). Morality consists of a pacific, truthful, upright and thoroughly disciplined way of life, reasoned to cause harm neither to oneself nor to others. For the Buddha's monks this meant a life of mendicancy, of poverty but not of self-mortification, of celibacy and of gentle honesty. Though the Buddha and his renunciant disciples elaborated a monastic disciplinary code consistent with Buddhist principles, this was probably in essence not far different from the code with which the Buddha began, a code inspired by the moral ideals then current among the wanderers and renouncers.

The second part of the path is meditation. Part of meditation is allied with morality: the attempt to restrain one's senses from what is immoral and to create good, wholesome and skilful frames of mind within which to work. The counterpart to this is the avoidance not only of bad actions but of bad frames of mind, which lead not to clarity but to delusion. Against this background the basic skill is concentration, coupled with equanimity, and this meditative control is then the basis of insight meditation. Insight meditation, however, is not practised only by sitting in quiet solitude. For it demands a general attitude of self-recollection, of clear consciousness, of awareness of one's surroundings, one's experiences, and one's actions and their consequences moment by moment, day by day. As it was taught to his pupils this meditative discipline is relatively systematised, but the Buddha fulfilled it unsystematically in the course of his search. These first two parts of the path could be thought of as a battery of skills rather like those of a painter: draftsmanship, the use of colour, the depiction of perspective and so forth. As these skills blend into a greater skill, that of painting itself, so all the individual exercises of morality and meditation blend into a single alert and calm way of life.

But the abilities of the painter must be wedded to a sensibility, a way of seeing the world. And analogously the third part of the path − wisdom − demands a radically new way of perceiving experience. One facet of this new perception is, quite simply, seeing the world as it is, and for the Buddha this meant seeing by means of the Four Noble Truths and dependent co-origination: in such-and-such a way is experience evanescent, devoid of abiding self and painfully flawed. In such-and-such a way does craving reproduce this suffering again and again.

The other facet is a <u>new attitude</u>, a new habit of mind, which grows out of the equanimity of meditation. One can now stand aloof from experience. One can see the dangers in it and turn away. One can observe, yet not pursue, even fleeting pleasures and aspirations as they flicker before the mind's eye. Perhaps the most compact statement of this sensibility is found in the stock prescription that the monk should 'not cling to the here and now, not grasp after situations, relinquish easily'. Or again:

[the monk] neither constructs in his mind, nor wills in order to produce, any state of mind or body, or the destruction of any such state. By not so willing anything in the world, he grasps after nothing; by not grasping, he is not anxious; he is therefore fully calmed within. (M III 244)

One should neither look forward to coming experiences, nor clutch at present ones, but let them all slip easily through one's fingers.

The Buddha took this to great lengths. In the Simile of the Raft (M I no. 22) he instances the case of a man who, faced by a flood, builds a raft from wood lying about and floats safely to the other side. The Buddha asks whether it would be rational for the man, having reached the other side, to put the raft on his head and carry it with him. The answer is that it would assuredly not be rational. Just so, concludes the Buddha, it is irrational to cling even to the profitable states of mind created by morality and meditation, still less to unprofitable states of mind. (This presupposes, of course, that through habituation and training the profitable practices are now second nature to the monk.) The same applies to ideas: to indulge in specula-tions and theories about the past or future, eternity, the fate of the world and so forth, is to lose oneself in 'a tangle of views, a thicket of views'. Instead one is to view the world simply, directly, with the perception achieved in insight meditation. This perception, like the artist's way of seeing, is highly cultivated, but it is nevertheless immediate and uncomplicated by reflection. One is to hover in a sensibility which the Buddha describes in one of his most poetic descriptions of liberation, where the flood refers to the painful stream of birth and death: 'if I stood still, I sank; if I struggled, I was carried away. Thus by neither standing still nor struggling, I crossed the flood' (S I l).

This is Nirvana, the 'blowing out' of the passions and frustrations of existence. The Buddha asserted that to speculate about the frame of mind of one thus awakened and liberated is to invite confusion and madness. But despite this useful advice, such speculation played a great part in subsequent Buddhist history, as it must in our assessment of the claims of Buddhism to our assent. The accounts of awakening in the canon foster the impression that one is either awakened or not, liberated or not, and that the switch from one to the other is practically instantaneous and irreversible. However, one of the issues in the first great schism in Buddhism, a few generations after the Buddha's death, was whether a liberated person can, even temporarily, backslide from awakening. And by the same token later schools conducted debates over whether awakening was instantaneous or gradual.

What these difficulties point to is a problem inherent in the language used in the canon to describe such impalpable matters: for the purposes of a narrative, the story of the Buddha's *awakening*, a sudden, dramatic and decisive transformation is required. And this is plausible to the extent that the awakening was a matter of certainty, of the knowledge that 'what was to be done has been done'. The Buddha realised that he had fulfilled all the requirements for liberation and no longer had to struggle arduously forward. But the *liberation* is a different matter, for here we are speaking of a wholesale transformation in the human constitution. It seems implausible that this transformation, as it is described in the canonical sources, could be other than gradual, a slow mastering of the whole wide field of one's behaviour and thought. In this respect the awakening had to be further certified and shown to be practically effective in the course of subsequent experience. We may accept that the Buddha was awakened one moon-lit night, but the liberation was an extended, indeed a life-long affair.

The question of whether the Buddha's notion of liberation is a believable or a practicable one must I think be answered in the affirmative. True, we cannot say anything useful about the claim that liberation puts an end to the rigours of death and rebirth. That is beyond our ability to argue cogently and bring evidence. But this claim is – as is so characteristic of the Buddha's style – linked to another more concrete claim, that liberation may be achieved in this life, and on this the Buddhist texts offer some grounds for discussion. It is not claimed that liberation puts an end to physical pain this side of the grave, for painfulness is admitted to be the nature of the body. (Someone accomplished in the Absorptions or Meditative Planes, however, might be able temporarily to anaesthetise himself by such meditation.) It is rather mental suffering, the extra and unnecessary anguish of existence, that is progressively dispelled by the Buddhist training. Moreover, the sources give us a relatively clear view of the effect of the training: the Buddha's monks 'do not repent the past nor brood over the future. They live in the present. Hence they are radiant' (S I 5).

The principle underlying the elaborate training is one

directed precisely to this end of living radiantly in the present. The Buddha called the principle 'thorough reflection' (*yoniso manasikāra*), a considered and meticulous pragmatism about the consequences of each practice in the Middle Path. 'For him who reflects thoroughly, cares and troubles which have not yet arisen do not arise, and those already arisen disappear' (M I 7). What this means in effect is that any practice must be seen to conduce to present welfare *as well as* to long-term transformation. There is no doubt a tension here. On the one hand, the monk's life is strenuous, and he must undertake practices which are at first quite uncomfortable. But on the other hand, since the practices are not designed as self-mortification, their fruits are not deferred indefinitely, but are witnessed and adjudged useful within a manageable period. What was difficult becomes second nature, an occasion not for anguish but for cool, indeed intellectually pleasurable, reflection on the nature and demands of experience in the mind and body. Furthermore, the monk is bolstered in this by the evaluation, repeatedly stressed in the texts, that such a life is not merely escape, but a noble and heroic vocation; and this evaluation is in turn certified by his fellow monks and by the surrounding society which prizes such fortitude.

Moreover, the present mastery of one field of the training not only produces benefits in itself, but also is seen as leading forward naturally to further mastery. Thus, for example, the monk's mastery of moral discipline produces a lack of remorse, a freedom from regret and anxiety. Because one commits no injury to oneself or others, one's conscience is clear, and this leads of itself to a serenity upon which meditative accomplishments may then be founded. This progressive mastery is considered to lead to the very summit, an aloofness from all the accidents of experience.

From our point of view what is important about this process

is its naturalness. One of the most intractable problems of a project such as the Buddha's is that desire is an enemy, but the final goal of liberation is one that the monk desires, wills. How is it possible to give up that impassioned will toward liberation itself? On the Buddha's account one wills the present object of training – e.g. to attain moral discipline – and the consequences fall into place. Thus, for example, 'there is no need for one well disciplined, endowed with moral discipline, to will with the intention "let me do away with remorse". For this is the way of things, O monks, that moral discipline does away with remorse' (A V 2). As one wills, and then relaxes into, each stage of practice the next stage is prepared. The final stage is attained not by strenuous willing at all, but by the now habitual relaxation.

The Buddha held the human constitution to be such that it could be laid bare to fruitful investigation through insight meditation and decisively transformed through the Buddhist training. The internal coherence of this view is difficult to fault, but our ultimate assent must be founded in experience, in empirical evidence. I can offer only my experience from field-work with meditating forest monks in contemporary Sri Lanka. Many monks were evidently healthy and content, 'radiant' and 'without remorse', and this in itself impressed me. Yet to be fair this may have been only the fruit of a quiet life, since I simply was not with any of the monks for the long years necessary to have witnessed and understood some slow metamorphosis of character through the Buddhist discipline.

There were, however, three traits of the monks which did seem directly pursuant upon the Buddhist training. The first was an interested, indeed fascinated, absorption in what they called their 'work', which referred to the hour-by-hour, minute-by-minute prosecution of the daily round – study, careful eating, hygiene, meditation, exercise – which makes up the monk's life. In the reflective execution of these ordinary tasks they clearly found tremendous satisfaction. But, second, some did nevertheless also pour tremendous energy and years of their lives into long-term projects, such as the founding of forest hermitages. Yet they still remained without anxiety and relatively indifferent to the results of their efforts. They were both remarkably successful and remarkably uninterested in success. These deep-seated attitudes were far enough from ordinary life and close enough to the Buddhist ideal of living in the present that I had no difficulty in attributing them to the monastic discipline.

It was the third trait, however, which most persuaded me of the discipline's effectiveness, and that was the monks' courage in the face of wild forest animals. On two occasions while on foot in the jungle there stood between me and a surprised and threatening animal – once a wild boar and once an elephant – only the slight body and unmoving equanimity of a monk. On both occasions the monk took a firm but unaggressive stance and spoke calmly to the animal, which crashed off into the underbrush. No behaviour could be further from ordinary expectations, and it attested vividly to the depth of transformation achievable through the Buddhist training. None of this, of course, proves the truth of the Buddha's teaching, but it does invite us to consider his philosophy seriously as one which has something to tell us about the nature and capacities of the human constitution.

5 The mission and the death

In the very long run Buddhism was strikingly successful: it became a world religion which until recently reigned over the Far East and mainland South-East Asia, the most populous areas of the globe, and now it is making its way in the West. However, we need only look a little closer to see that this is not to be explained simply as the triumphant progress of the truth. In the Buddha's time and for many centuries afterwards in India his teaching competed with others on a more of less equal footing. It was not until the middle of the first millennium after Christ, ten to fifteen centuries after the Buddha, that its hegemony was firmly established in the rest of Asia, and shortly thereafter it was on its way to extinction in India itself. Buddhism's history is one of many different episodes, and in each episode different social, economic and political factors – factors often quite extraneous to Buddhism – have played a part. So even if we agree that the Buddha's teaching was insightful and practicable, these virtues alone can hardly in themselves be regarded as the motive force in Buddhism's successes.

Nevertheless, Buddhism did have properties which, if they did not actively motivate Buddhism's expansion, did at least make that expansion possible. The evidence of these is found in Buddhism's relatively easy adaptation to other, native religious traditions in the areas it colonised. Buddhism coexisted with archaic Hinduism in India and Sri Lanka, Taoism and Confucianism in China, the Bon religion in Tibet and Shinto in Japan. Indeed Buddhism is presently adapting to Marxism in the East and to liberal humanism and liberal

Christianity in the West. In all these circumstances it has been possible for Buddhists to cleave to indigenous beliefs for certain worldly, religious or civil purposes, while simultaneously holding Buddhist views about their own psychological nature and the ultimate ends of human action. Buddhism, in other words, has had little of the imperiousness which has characterised missionary religions such as Christianity and Islam. It is quintessentially tolerant, cosmopolitan and portable, and hence it has been able to respond to opportunities created by circumstances quite beyond its control.

The foundations of this portability lie in three interconnected features of the Buddha's own teaching. First, it was explicitly directed to human beings by virtue of characteristics they held in common: the capacity for pleasure and suffering, the ability to affect their own and others' welfare. One could, of course, object that other Indian religions, and indeed other world religions, embodied similar attempts to speak to all humanity. But, second, in the Buddha's case this universalistic project was relatively good at actually being universalistic because it was abstract. We have seen this abstraction at work, for example, in the Buddha's description of the Absorptions, a description which is consistent with many systems of meditation and with different purposes in meditation. And in the same spirit the Buddha's conception of wisdom and virtue neither opposed nor condoned India's nascent caste system, but rather spoke of human action in abstract terms which were indifferent to the presence or absence of caste: it could exist within or without caste society. Third, this abstraction was always linked in the Buddha's teaching with a deliberately limited concern to apply it to the structure of individual human experience alone. There was a great deal about the world upon which he simply refused to pronounce. Hence, on the one hand, it has always been possible for people to agree in

Buddhism while living in quite different culture
quite different views about the world. And on the o
has been possible for Buddhists themselves in the
history to add to the Buddha's own teaching the most
doctrines – doctrines which fitted in with local tradition.
circumstances.

However, this leaves unanswered one fundamental and
troublesome question. As I have so far described the Buddha's
teaching it is really directed only to that handful who are
willing and able to pursue the life of a monk with total devo-
tion. Yet the acceptance of Buddhism by whole peoples meant
that it was embraced by a laity who did not 'go forth from
home into homelessness'. How did Buddhism develop from a
teaching for the few into a teaching for the many? What did
this élitist message have to offer people in the world? These
questions were answered in the course of the Buddha's career
after the awakening.

The most plausible accounts of the Buddha's life before and
during the awakening are found in bare and simple narratives
in which the Buddha seems to speak of his own experience. It
is easy to accept that these have an ancestry, however distant,
in edifying discourses the Buddha actually imparted to his
monks. In contrast, the oldest legends of the Buddha's life
after the awakening (I speak here and hereafter of the
beginning of *Mahāvagga*) are in the third person, evidently
took form some generations after the Buddha's death, and are
full of mythical detail. They are therefore far from trust-
worthy. They do, however, convey at least some sense of how
the Buddha's personal liberation was metamorphosed into a
mission to the world at large.

The seed of the Buddha's mission is wrapped in an especially mythic guise in the legend. While the Buddha was still
mulling over in solitude the consequences of his discoveries,

81

he decided that it would be pointless and tiresome to announce them to a world sunk in ignorance. But a god intervened: as is characteristic in Buddhist legend, the god is merely a walk-on character who supports the central plot of human self-transformation. He pleaded to the Buddha on behalf of all those creatures who had 'only a little dust in their eyes', who would respond well and gratefully to the Buddha's message. To this plea the Buddha responded generously, undertaking to spread abroad his remedy for suffering, 'out of compassion for creatures'. And thus was born that resolve which Buddhists regard as bringing light to the world's darkness.

The truth of the matter is impossible to discern, but this legendary vignette is nevertheless revealing. In the first place, it points to a fundamental feature of the Buddha's mature teaching, that it embodied not only the governing value of liberation, but also the second governing value of compassion: concern for others. And indeed something like compassion was inherent in the Buddha's moral seriousness and in his propensity for describing the mind in moral terms, in terms of the effects of mental actions on others. Compassion for the Buddha was intimately intertwined with liberation as a human purpose and guiding sentiment. However, in the legend compassion has a significance narrower than it and its corollaries were to have in the elaborated teaching. Here compassion is a personal attribute of the Buddha and the sufficient motive for his decision to teach. Moreover it is a compassion directed to a specific end, the imparting of the Buddha's version of the renunciant life.

A good deal of this section of the legendary biography is concerned with the consequences of this compassion, the formation of an order of monks following the Buddha. The Buddha arose from solitude and wandered by stages to the city of Benares, where he stayed in the Deer Park at Isipatana. There he met five ascetics who had been with him before the awakening, but who had left in disgust when he gave up self-mortification. To them he addressed his first sermon, the Setting in Motion of the Wheel of the Teaching, which enunciated the Middle Path and the Four Noble Truths. This they accepted, they became his disciples, and from that time on many of his converts were drawn from the body of wanderers and ascetics. This is historically plausible to the extent that many of the Buddha's discourses were addressed to such wanderers, who were at the time a fluid group, moving easily from one teacher to another. But what was now at stake was the foundation of a new and enduring institution, the Order (*sangha*) of monks following the Buddha, and indeed one senses that the general fluidity was now crystallising everywhere into separate religious corporations with their own constitutions.

However, the Buddha was addressing an audience broader than just the religious virtuosi. The next convert was Yasa, a rich young layman, who awoke one morning suddenly filled with disgust at the sight of the courtesans with whom he had taken his pleasure, now lying about him in drunken slumber. He wandered disconsolately to the Deer Park, and there he met the Buddha, who announced to him the Four Noble Truths. So Yasa left the world to join the Buddha and his small band. Yasa was a merchant's son, and according to the legend four of Yasa's friends 'from the leading merchant families of Benares' then became disciples, and then a further fifty 'youths from the countryside'. These were the kernel of the new Order, and indeed it was they who spread the teaching abroad: for in the legend the Buddha now adjured them to 'go out and wander for the well-being and happiness of the many, out of compassion for the world . . .'. But they were no Protestant evangelists creating a church of laymen, for they were to 'propound the absolutely perfect and wholly pure life of celibate mendicancy'.

Certain elements of this ring true. There was an elective affinity between Buddhism and city merchants, who were among the founding members of the complex urbane society which the Buddha's teaching addressed. But his was also a universal message, and many besides merchants − perhaps the youths 'of the countryside' − must also have joined the Order. The emphasis on the celibate life seems especially plausible, for it expressed the *esprit de corps* of the Order, and it is consistent with the message of many of the discourses, that the only truly rational course is to renounce the world. However, even if this uncompromising purpose was the original brief of the Order, the missionary activity held within it the possibility of a profound involvement with the laity: for it was after all the laymen's food which sustained, and their cloth which protected the mendicant missionaries as they spread along the trade routes through India and later throughout Asia.

So laymen do appear in the legendary biography. Immediately after Yasa joined the Order, Yasa's father came looking for him and met the Buddha, who preached to him. The father was converted, 'he gained confidence' in the Buddha's teaching, and he thereupon 'went for refuge to the Buddha as long as breath lasts'. This 'going for refuge' today marks formally a layman's commitment to the Buddha, his Order and his teaching, and it seems likely that it had a similar significance at the time of the compilation of the legend and earlier. Yasa's father then invited the Buddha for a meal, and while at the father's home the Buddha converted Yasa's former wife and his mother as well, who also 'went for refuge' to the Buddha. These events at Yasa's father's home convey the substance of the relationship between Buddhist monks and laymen. The laymen offer food and physical support to the monks, while the monks offer the laymen wisdom and other spiritual goods. Anthropologists are fond of discovering institutions based on long-term gift exchange, in which two parties establish a relationship by giving gifts to each other and continue the relationship by the continued exchange of gifts, and this is such a case. On the laymen's part liberality, and especially generosity towards monks, is enjoined, whereas on the monk's side 'the gift of the Buddha's teaching is the best gift', as the canon repeatedly asserts. The gifts are different in kind, but they are given freely, and through them lasting ties are created. Upon this mutual exchange there was thus formed the Buddhist community as a whole, the 'fourfold assembly', which included monks, nuns (whom the Buddha later sanctioned), laymen and laywomen. It was this community as a whole that achieved Buddhism's lasting success.

So what the Buddha's teaching had to offer the laity was certain spiritual goods. Some of these goods were not offered by Buddhism alone, however. One was merit, an immaterial reward garnered by a layman simply by feeding a monk and listening to his sermon. Merit could be laid up to secure a better rebirth: the more merit in the spiritual account, so to speak, the better the rebirth. Hence, as there was a high spiritual purpose appropriate to the monk, namely liberation, so there was a lower one appropriate to the layman, better rebirth (and the hope that one would eventually be reborn in circumstances allowing one to become a monk and achieve liberation). This was a good reason for patronising the Buddhist Order; but in fact it was also a reason for patronising others such as the Jain order as well, for they too held a similar conception of merit.

Another spiritual good offered to the laity was a high moral teaching, composed of injunctions against such acts as lying, killing and stealing; against gaining one's livelihood in harmful ways; and against destructive attitudes of greed, hatred and folly. The monk, with his strenuous discipline of self-control, represented the perfection of human virtue, but the basic principles of that perfection were adaptable to a lower level, to a morality fitting the compromised circumstances of a laity who had to make their living and bear their children in the world. The Buddha, however, held no monopoly of such teachings, whose novelty and popularity were linked with the relative newness and wide distribution of the now developing urbanized forms of social life. Now there were merchants who, through command of the impersonal instruments of money and trade, could wreak a new damage on others; now there were states and armies with new capabilities of harm; now there were offices to seek at others' expense. Moreover, life in the new cities required that groups who had no natural mutual interest or mutually inherited moral code had to devise ways of living together with at least a bare minimum of trust. Much of the adaptation to new forms of life must have occurred quite apart from the renouncers, but the renouncers gave form and voice to the change. They embodied the virtues of harmlessness and poverty (the Buddha's monks were not even to touch gold or silver). They sought no offices. And in their preaching they advocated virtues whose practice – whatever theory went with them – could render the new social world habitable.

The teachings of merit and lay morality explain the renouncers', and not merely the Buddha's, success. Indeed in ancient India Buddhism would probably seldom have seemed markedly more successful than other movements, and taken singly many of the Buddha's teachings to the laity could be found in other doctrines. However, the Buddha achieved a synthesis of the various elements which made the whole more than the sum of the parts. This synthesis is formed upon the

Buddha's tendency to think in practical terms, on the analogy of craftsmanship, and also upon his concern with psychological explanations.

The key to this way of thinking is embodied in a term found frequently in his discourses. This term is *kusala,* whose primary meaning is 'skilful', as a goldsmith may be skilful at making gold ornaments. It is a term which the Buddha made his own, and he used it in the first place to refer to skill in meditation. But he also used it widely to apply to skill in moral discipline and in the acquisition of merit. In this application 'skilful' also means morally good, as we might say 'he is a good man' or 'that was a good act'. Indeed in many contexts 'skilful' is the opposite of evil, and refers to the same kind of sharp distinction that is made in Christianity between good and evil. But for the Buddha 'skilful/good' always had a practical, not a metaphysical or absolute flavour to it. The dead centre of the term is best conveyed by a sense lost to us (but still alive among the ancient Greeks), that just as one could be skilful or *good at* a craft, so one could be *good at* being a sentient being, and hence one could be *good.*

This term was animated by 'thorough reflection' upon the consequences of deeds and in particular of the attitudes, the mental actions, behind deeds. For the Buddha skilfulness cut two ways: its consequences were good for oneself, but good for others as well. For example, the act of giving food to a monk gained one merit, and indeed with the characteristic Buddhist emphasis upon the mental side of things this merit was conceived as being also a psychological good, a wholesome frame of mind pursuant upon liberality. But giving is also good for the monk, at the very least because the monk thereby assuages his hunger. By the same token, to cultivate moral discipline is simultaneously to avoid harm to others and to create good/skilful frames of mind in oneself. We tend to think of doing good as involving the sacrifice of one's own interests for someone else's, but for the Buddha to do good was precisely to act in both one's own *and* in someone else's interest. For the monk the stress was on one's own interest, liberation, while the means – exemplary moral discipline – incidentally achieved others' interests. But this way of thought was easily turned around to apply to laymen, who by being good to others achieved the end of being good to themselves. This reasoning was further bolstered by the teaching that to be kind, gentle, honest and harmless to others was in fact to invite them to behave in the same manner to oneself: do good to others that they may do good to you. By wise reflection and moral action Buddhists, whether monks or laymen, could achieve the fruit of their skilfulness 'both here and in the next world'.

The Buddha's doctrine for laymen, therefore, was intimately and organically connected to his thought on his monks' training. But this connection was not limited to the level of morality alone. For the monk the moral discipline underpins cultivation of the mind in meditation; but for both monks and laymen the cultivation of certain mental skills and attitudes could in turn underpin morality. It is here that compassion, concern for others, enters the picture again, now as an attitude to be cultivated meditatively and as a value directed to others' welfare in general. One can transform oneself not only for liberation, but also for love. In the Buddhist texts compassion is analysed into three: first, compassion proper, defined as sympathy with others' suffering; second, sympathetic joy, the enjoyment of others' good fortune; and third, loving-kindness, the Buddhist sentiment *par excellence*. The attitude cultivated by monks and laymen in loving-kindness is expressed in this famous passage of very early Buddhist poetry:

Whatever beings may exist — weak or strong, tall, broad, medium or short, fine-material or gross, seen or unseen, those born and those pressing to be born — may they all without exception be happy in heart!

Let no one deceive anyone else, nor despise anyone anywhere. May no one wish harm to another in anger or ill-will!

Let one's thoughts of boundless loving-kindness pervade the whole world, above, below, across, without obstruction, without hatred, without enmity! (S 146–8, 150)

This passage compresses the attitudes underlying the morality taught by the Buddha into a single sentiment, capturing the positive spirit that is to accompany the negative injunctions. Indeed loving-kindness is absolutely necessary both in the monk's training and in the lay morality, since for Buddhists it is the mental action, the intention or attitude, which counts and not the deed itself. The sentiment of loving-kindness is certainly impersonal, and in this the Olympian detachment of the renouncer shows through. One must treat all equally, regardless of position or relationship. Indeed in this universal sentiment the Buddha's moral reasoning has a place, for in prescriptions for loving-kindness the meditator is to 'identify oneself with all' (A II 129). That is, just as I am subject to pain and pleasure, so are others, and just as I wish myself well, so I should wish well to others. Throughout the Buddhist world loving-kindness, supplemented by compassion for suffering, was to become the model for social sentiments beyond the family and a value in its own right. In later Buddhist folklore and thought these sentiments grew so prominent as to over-shadow even the premier value of liberation.

*

The assembled structure of the Buddha's teaching to laymen is revealed in the Discourse to the Kālāmans (A I 188–93), a people on the northern fringe of the Gangetic civilisation. In that discourse the Buddha is represented as touring with a body of monks through the area. A group of Kālāmans learn of his presence and go to him in the village of Kesaputta with a problem. various wandering ascetics and Brahmans have travelled through expounding and recommending their own views to the Kālāmans, while attacking and rebutting the views of others. The Kālāmans are confused, and seek advice from the Buddha. Whom should they believe? To this confusion the Buddha replies with a teaching which has frequently been quoted to demonstrate the Buddha's lack of dogmatism and advocacy of individual judgment. He asserts that the Kālāmans should not rely on 'hearsay, on tradition, on legends, on learning, nor on mere inference or extrapolation or cogitation, nor on consideration and approval of some theory or other, nor because it seems fitting, nor out of respect for some ascetic'.

This is not a recommendation for capricious individual fancy, however, for what the Buddha recommends is his own moral reasoning from wise reflection and skilfulness, and he is confident that if the Kālāmans so reason they will each one arrive at the Buddha's moral teaching:

when you know for yourselves that this is unskilful and that skilful, this blameworthy and that blameless, this deprecated by the wise because it conduces to suffering and ill, and that praised because it conduces to well-being and happiness . . . when you know this for yourselves, Kālāmans, you will reject the one and make a practice of the other.

The moral teaching at which they will arrive is a straightforward one. The Kālāmans will not kill, they will not take what is not given, they will not take another's wife, they will not incite others to their own harm. These injunctions will arise naturally out of the Kālāmans' experience and their reflection upon skilfulness.

In the first place it is possible to infer a certain topicality in the discourse. There is reason to believe that the Kālāmans, like their neighbours the Sakyans, the Buddha's people, had had an independent oligarchic republican government and had been, in the remembered past, a relatively autonomous people. But now they were subjected to the power of the Kosalan king, as the Sakyans were soon to be, and in their economic life they must have felt the magnetic pull of the distant Kosalan capital. These political and economic forces were drawing the Kālāmans out of a relatively simple and closed tribal society into the complex world of Gangetic civilisation, and these dislocations were compounded by new cultural forms, embodied in the conflicting advice of those messengers of the Gangetic civilisation, the wandering ascetics.

It is impossible to believe that the injunctions against killing, lying, stealing and so forth were wholly new to the Kālāmans: their own ancestral culture must have offered analogous injunctions. It is difficult to conceive the survival of a society which did not hold these values in some form, at least as touches the members of the society itself. However, it is characteristic of societies like the older Kālāman one that such values are not reasoned, but are rather held by virtue of tradition and custom, and dramatised in legend and ritual. Under the new conditions these inherited moral traditions had lost their unquestioned hegemony, though, and hence there was occasion for the Buddha to offer a new form of moral reasoning which grew out of the most basic conditions of human life. The proposed morality was not a specifically Kālāman thing, but grew out of the sheer fact of being in society at all, of having a common life, of being able to reason for one's own

91

and others' ends, whoever was involved. This morality was meant to hold for all conditions.

But the Buddha envisaged more than just a new foundation for Kālāman morality. For the injunctions are meant to apply not only within Kālāman society, but to all individuals, Kālāman or not, with whom a Kālāman might deal: and the Kālāmans were already implicated with many other peoples. It is typical of small-scale societies, and of small groups within a larger society, that their members alone are treated as full constituents of the moral community. But now the Kālāmans were invited into a larger world to embrace within their moral community all living beings, and certainly all the people of the Gangetic plain. The Buddha promulgated a universal morality to fit the Kālāmans' enforcedly more cosmopolitan life.

To this extent the Buddha's teaching to laymen was founded on his moral reasoning, but in the discourse this moral reasoning is in turn founded more deeply in his teaching and experience, in his analysis of the human constitution and his project for self-transformation. When he taught the monks the Buddha emphasised that the sources of suffering – greed, hatred, delusion – lead to one's own harm. But in this teaching to laymen he stressed that they are generally harmful, not only harmful to oneself.

When greed rises within a man does it not conduce to harm? Or when hatred and delusion arise within a man? Is it not when his mind is overcome with greed, hatred, and delusion that a man murders, steals, lies, and so forth? And is it not by having a mind unconquered by these things that he is able to avoid all these acts?

In this passage 'harm' refers to harm caused both to oneself and to others: just as to be skilful is to serve both one's own ends and others' ends, so to be harmful is to harm both oneself and others. The point is worth emphasising, because not only Westerners but also later schools of Buddhism have wished to reject or improve on the Buddha's teaching on the grounds that it is oblivious to others' welfare or to the existence of society. Although on balance the Buddha was more concerned with the anatomy of individual experience than with the anatomy of society, his teaching always recognised that to be human is to be a social being.

Moreover the Buddha's view of how a layman is to mend himself so that his mind is 'unconquered' relies on more than just wise reflection. On the one hand, the Buddha presupposes in laymen a rational faculty which, if rightly directed, will produce skilful solutions to moral problems. Laymen can calculate what to do. But on the other hand this view of laymen as having a capacity for rationality is only part of the story, for the Buddha also felt that laymen could – to an extent appropriate to their station – transform themselves. Hence in the Discourse to the Kālāmans the Buddha recommends the meditation on the social sentiments, especially loving-kindness. Laymen are to practise by directing loving-kindness to all quarters and all beings, 'identifying oneself with all . . . having a heart free of anger and hatred'. The effect of this mental exercise is to establish loving-kindness sooner or later as a lasting habit and motivation in action.

This has two important implications. First, it means that the Buddha recommended not only *why* one should act skilfully, but also *how* the sometimes intractable human constitution can be made to do so. The Buddha was an optimist in that he thought humans capable of skilful rationality, but a realist in that he knew this rationality to require an emotional transformation as well. One may calculate an act to be good and skilful, and yet be unable to carry it out, and this common weakness was taken fully into account. Second, this practice of

93

self-transformation is portable, in the sense that in principle it may be practised effectively by anyone. This is important because much of human experience, and especially that beyond the bounds of an enclosed group such as the Buddhist Order, cannot be manipulated to one's own ends. The Kālāmans were subject to natural changes but also, and increasingly, to social changes which were beyond anyone's power to control or even to understand fully. But here at least was a matter which one could effectively handle: one's own habits and motivations. If one cannot change the world, one can at least change oneself. True, a practice for laymen such as the meditation on loving-kindness must be partly dependent for its effectiveness on one's being part of a Buddhist community which cleaves to such values; but the final effort is one's own and the focus of effort is oneself. A Kālāman travelling to the Kosalan capital or a Kālāman working his ancestral fields could both equally well practise loving-kindness and compassion.

The Discourse to the Kālāmans is perhaps quite topical, but as the Buddha phrased it the discourse, like many of his other teachings to laymen, is applicable to anyone in a similar plight. In this the Buddha is strikingly modern, for today it is difficult to find a people which has not been drawn into a wider, more complex, more confusing social world, as the Kālāmans were drawn into Gangetic civilisation. The Buddha addressed himself by the very generality of his discourse to the wide variety of possible fates in the experience of a complex society, and that experience of complexity is ours at least as much as it was the ancient Indians'. On the surface people now, as then, obey the dictates of a bewildering variety of different necessities and values, but there are some traits which they all share: the capacity for misery or happiness, the capacity to harm or benefit others.

Indeed this modernity corresponds to certain hard-won views of our own. The Buddha was original in his consciousness of the varieties of culture in his milieu, and he was capable of recommending in the canon, for example, that different groups adhere each to its own ancestral morality and religion. The Buddha recognised, that is, that peoples' values are relative to their own history and culture. We too have come to recognise this irreducible difference of values: we call it cultural relativism, and we take this to mean that other societies are not to be judged by our own. But just as cultural relativism cannot realistically be thought to mean that people can live according to just any values or with no values, so the Buddha advocated that people adhere to ancestral standards *only in so far as* those standards are consistent with moral skilfulness. Similarly the Buddha taught that human individuals are not to be seen as isolated from each other, but as conjoined to each other in a weighty and consequential relationship. This is consistent with another modern view, a growing awareness that individuals are not to be understood in isolation, but as being inextricably involved in a social context.

There is another kind of modernity, however, which the Buddha did not have, and that is an overriding preoccupation with the political dimension of human affairs. For the most part the Buddha's discourses define three areas of concern which, between them, make up the human world as it is seen by the Buddha: an individual's concern with the events of his own mind and body, his concern with his face-to-face personal relations with others, and his concern with the welfare of all sentient beings. For these three areas, the psychic, the socially very small-scale, and the universal collectivity of all beings, he was willing to lay down both the way things are and the way they should be. But these descriptions and prescriptions say little about how men do and should behave as members of

95

political collectivities, and how political collectivities should be organised. Certainly this relative indifference to the specifics of political affairs must have contributed to the ease with which the Buddha's teaching has been found relevant in very different political climates.

But this is not to say that the Buddha's teaching is devoid of political interest or political implications. In so far as we can infer the Buddha's own preferences, they were for the sort of oligarchic egalitarian or republican political organisation that seems to have held among his own people. And we know this because his prescriptions for the organisation of the Buddhist Order, which appear in a long biographical text on his last days, are set beside very similar prescriptions for another such people. The Order (or the people) are to conduct their business in concord, their decisions are to be unanimous, they are to respect and defer to elders, but where elders' views conflict with the teaching and disciplinary code (or the tradition of the group), one is to follow the teaching. Had such oligarchies prospered and expanded, we might have had ancient Indian theories of democracy and citizenship such as ancient Greece gave us. But oligarchies had probably never been the principal form of government in India: they were very much on their way out when the Buddha lived, and very soon they were gone forever. Most of the Buddha's experience was with kingdoms, and no king wishes to hear radical political thought.

So the Buddha was left to talk about kings if he was to talk about politics at all. There are left to us a number of fascinating discourses which must have taken their complex literary form after the Buddha's death but some of which quite possibly represent the Buddha's views, and in these he expounds on kingship. The chief message is that kings, no less than anyone else, are subject to the moral order, to considerations of what is morally and socially skilful. When there came to be

Buddhist kings these discourses were taken at face value to construct a specifically Buddhist theory of ethical kingship. Other messages include what seems to be a recommendation for state capitalism, to the effect that the king should finance enterprises in order to bring prosperity to the people; and a contract theory of the monarchy, to the effect that the king is elected because he is the handsomest and best and able to keep people in line. But these messages are set in highly ironical and even humorous frames, in which the Buddha tells a fanciful story to an imaginary figure (e.g. Sharptooth the Brahman), and the consequence is that the Buddha is distanced very far from the messages he seems to convey. Part of this distancing is that of a world renouncer looking down from the perspective of liberation upon the folly and pettiness of even grand state affairs. But there is a keen edge to this commentary which implies that the Buddha must have been a very perspicacious observer of the political scene.

In the light of our deeply disillusioning experience of the teachings of the past as they have been applied in the world, we might very well doubt that any past master still bears cogency and relevance. And one might further object in the case of the Buddha that his mastery is not *world-wide*, but is grounded upon views of the cosmos, such as transmigration, which can never be accepted by the West. But I have tried to show that the philosophy of the Buddha was concerned with matters that do make his mastery available to everyone, that do bring him within Western history, though the West must – quite appropriately – expand its view of its own history beyond parochial preoccupations to embrace him. The Buddha was concerned with the physical and psychological bases upon which human self-transformation is possible: such a mastery could not be lost to us. His teaching was suited to a world of different political philosophies and different religions, but a world in which certain basic values must guide personal relations if we are to live together at all, and it is difficult to see how that mastery could be irrelevant to us.

The story of the Buddha's death is recounted in a long text (D II no. 16) which, shorn of its mythical elements, portrays the last journey of an old man. Accompanied by his now continual companion, the loving but, as the text portrays him, rather bumbling Ānanda, the Buddha made his way northward over hundreds of miles, plagued by illness. Finally the Buddha was struck down by food poisoning and came to rest in the obscure village of Kusinārā.

When Ānanda realised that the Buddha was about to die, 'he went into a house and leaned against the doorframe weeping'. The Buddha called Ānanda to himself and told him,

do not mourn, do not weep. Haven't I told you that we are separated, parted, cut off from everything dear and beloved? . . . You have served me long with love, helpfully, gladly, sincerely and without reserve, in body, word, and thought. You have done well by yourself, Ānanda. Keep trying and you will soon be liberated.

Further Reading

A great deal has been published in English about Buddhism, some of it very technical, some of it misleading and some of it very good indeed. These are suggestions which will lead to a more comprehensive understanding of the Buddha, of his teaching, and of the history of Buddhism.

Quite a different approach to the Buddha's biography was taken by Bhikkhu Ñāṇamoḷi in *The Life of the Buddha* (Buddhist Publication Society, Kandy, 1972), which is available from the Society in Kandy, Sri Lanka. He tells the story of the Buddha entirely through accurate translations from the Pali texts themselves. This book is perhaps the best introduction to the Pali texts, with their peculiarly meticulous and laconic style. Yet another approach was taken by Michael Pye in *The Buddha* (Duckworth, 1979). He conveys a vivid sense of the Buddha's life as well as of the stories and myths through which the early Buddhist community came to see the Buddha. Both of these would very usefully supplement the picture I have given.

For the Buddha's teaching there is nothing better than Walpola Rahula's *What the Buddha Taught* (Gordon Fraser, 1967). This combines lucidity with a warm advocacy of Buddhism from the point of view of a practising monk. Nyanaponika Thera has written a similarly lucid book on insight meditation, *The Heart of Buddhist Meditation* (Rider, 1969). These are both based on the Theravāda tradition.

For a broader introduction to the breadth of Buddhist philosophy and history Richard Robinson and Willard L. Johnson's book, *The Buddhist Religion* (Dickenson, 1982) is especially good. This may then be followed by Heinz Bechert and Richard Gombrich (eds.), *The World of Buddhism* (Thames and Hudson, 1984), which is composed of articles on Buddhism and the Buddhist order in each of the Buddhist countries. Though written for a general readership each article represents the latest scholarship on each area.

It would be well to supplement such reading with an acquaintance with the Buddhist texts themselves, which can be consulted in Henry C. Warren's *Buddhism in Translations* (Atheneum, 1963) or in Stephen Beyer's more recent *Buddhist Experience: Sources and Interpretations* (Dickenson, 1974).

Many of these books have useful bibliographies which will then lead the reader further into the subject he or she wishes to study. My own interest has been in the actual practice of Buddhism in Buddhist lands today. On this Holmes Welch's *The Practice of Chinese Buddhism, 1900–1950* (Harvard University Press, 1967) is particularly thorough. My own understanding of Buddhism is based on field work in Sri Lanka, and I have written of that in *The Forest Monks of Sri Lanka* (Oxford University Press, 1983). This picture of strict meditative practitioners is complemented by Richard Gombrich's *Precept and Practice* (Oxford University Press, 1971), which concerns the beliefs and practices of popular Buddhism in Sri Lanka.

Index

Compiled by Patricia Utechin

Index